# Survive & Thrive

*Dating and being single*

A *Self Help Guide* to building resilience, confidence, making the most of single life and believing in you just as you are.

*Jennifer Boon*

Copyright © 2017 Jennifer Boon

The moral right of the author has been asserted.

Apart from any fair dealing for the purposes of research or private study, or criticism or review, as permitted under the Copyright, Designs and Patents Act 1988, this publication may only be reproduced, stored or transmitted, in any form or by any means, with the prior permission in writing of the publishers, or in the case of reprographic reproduction in accordance with the terms of licences issued by the Copyright Licensing Agency. Enquiries concerning reproduction outside those terms should be sent to the publishers.

Matador
9 Priory Business Park,
Wistow Road, Kibworth Beauchamp,
Leicestershire. LE8 0RX
Tel: 0116 279 2299
Email: books@troubador.co.uk
Web: www.troubador.co.uk/matador
Twitter: @matadorbooks

ISBN 978 1788033 206

British Library Cataloguing in Publication Data.
A catalogue record for this book is available from the British Library.

Printed by TJ International, Padstow, Cornwall, UK
Typeset in 11pt Aldine401 BT by Troubador Publishing Ltd, Leicester, UK

Matador is an imprint of Troubador Publishing Ltd

*This book is dedicated to my soul mate Si.
Thank you for your constant love, encouragement and belief in me.
You are and always will be my one true love.*

# Contents

Introduction vii
Making this book work for you xiii

## Creating your I-can-handle-anything foundation  1

1. Turning a spotlight on what's going on in your life, right now  3
2. Bouncing Back  32
3. Let's start with loving you  54
4. Empowering you to make the most of your life right now  78

## Relying on you Section  95

5. Trusting and Using your Intuition  97
6. You're fab, believe it!
   Your confidence-boosters  109

# Date-smart     119

7. Dating words of wisdom     121
8. Dating – Preparing for your date/
  tapping in to your inner dating goddess     131
9. Date Smart     135
10. Internet dating     148
11. Break Up Survival Support –
  how to survive and be sassier     158

Afterword     171
Acknowledgements     173

# Introduction
## Beginning our journey together

Hello there! This book is all about the ins and outs of finding love and how to survive and thrive on the rollercoaster of craziness and excitement (and at times pain and heartache) in finding *the one*!

This book will equip you with the skills you need to get through this stage without going crazy questioning yourself – 'is it me?' It's a self-help practical guide, pulling on my experience as a life coach and using my background in positive psychology. But I also share my journey in finding love. This book will help guide you through the highs and lows of love, be there to pick you up when you get down, and to grow you into the amazing woman that you know deep down you are. This book will arm you with resilience, strengthen your skills in intuition, and arm you with visioning tools to help *you* create the life you want with or without a partner.

I have been on a whirlwind journey through the dating years. From being in monogamous relationships to being in dating scarcity, first date overload right through to now being very happily married to my soulmate. It was a rollercoaster to say the least and many times along the way I didn't think I would make it out the other end. I tried different approaches, from not focusing on love to fully focusing on it, to acceptance, to asking outright to the universe – what on earth is going on! So let's get started on this journey! Hold on tight!

The seed of the idea of this book came about many years ago (seven to be precise) when I was retelling yet another first-date disaster to my work colleague at the time, Wendy. I regularly entertained the team with my dating disasters and one day my lovely friend suggested I start writing about my experiences as I had so many hideous and hilarious encounters. I didn't think much of it, but it had started growing a seed of an idea about what I had learnt and what I was learning through dating. I'd had pretty much every horrendous situation under the sun with dating and yes it was hilarious to recount the stories back, but there was a big part of me that thought 'why me?' Why haven't I found someone yet? Where is my soulmate? Why is he taking so bloomin' long to get here?!! I have a timeline to follow! Where is he? And the longer he took to materialise the more disheartened I found myself.

Dating taught me how to love me regardless of what was going on out there and whatever man was rejecting me, it taught me to pick myself up and shine. I want to share this with you, because dating can be fun, but it can also be lonely and horrible and depressing. And when, for the umpteenth time, you find a weekend looming that is scarily empty or a friend cancels at the last minute without realising she *was* your weekend plans, it can feel like a losing game of musical chairs – with you being left with no chair.

To give you context as to why I am writing this book, my story went something like this; I started dating at fourteen years old, and was pretty much in various long-term relationships until just before my thirtieth birthday. Around this time, I was dumped rather hideously by a boyfriend who I thought I was moving in with, who one evening, started breaking down in tears (before dumping me). I thought something had happened to a family member I had *no idea* I was about to be dumped. I had only the hour before been on the phone to my sister gushing about moving in and looking for houses. Forward wind an hour and I was weeping down the phone to my sister, and my brother was in his car on his way round to pick up the pieces of yet another dating disaster. This was the biggy for me – I had always had a dream, goal and a deadline to be married by thirty and that deadline was fast looming. I looked back over my dating life to that point and realised I had barely had a time of more than a couple of months when I had had a chance to be single and not in the throws of some relationship. I had absolutely no idea who I was and had joked up to that point about the fact I always seemed to have a boyfriend – but it was getting kind of a ridiculous pattern. This last boyfriend, let's call him 'Mr Dramatic Exit' man, was the straw that broke the camel's back so to speak.

After being dumped, I vowed to take a year out of dating and focus on me: my wants and needs and to spend time looking after me. So I began a journey of self discovery. The universe was trying to tell me something and I obviously wasn't listening! The lessons were getting more and more dramatic so that finally I had to stop and listen. I needed time on my own away from dating. I was scared and going cold turkey was not much fun. I didn't really know who I was. I reflected how I had often merged with my partners' wants and needs and dreams without thinking about my own.

As my thirtieth birthday loomed I faced the sobering reality that unless my soulmate was going to miraculously drop out of the sky, I was not going to be happily married with a baby on the way by thirty.

This realisation was hard to take. I cried and dramatically

asked, 'why me?' Luckily I had an amazing group of friends to nurture me and help me survive my nightmare of being single and hitting the big 3-0.

With my time out of dating I did something for me. I got braces: train tracks top and bottom with the additional fashion accessory of dental elastics to keep the jaw in alignment. It was something I had been put off of by previous boyfriends, but this was now for me, purely for me. I revelled in this. I started looking at myself both inside and out and felt fear and excitement when I started thinking about what I wanted. I believe your body gives you certain messages until you decide to listen. For me it was my hair. It had been getting thinner and thinner and I had been ignoring it. This was my moment to take time out and get back to the important business of me.

I took time to reflect and put myself out there. I didn't have loads of friends in London and had never really invested in my friendships although I was lucky that I had developed some amazing friendships despite this. My early to mid thirties were spent lurching between dating and not – and I found that dating was certainly no picnic. I found I had to trust my intuition like no time before and I had to keep picking myself up. I started to understand me and what my wants and likes were and looked under my belief bonnet to figure out what I was all about. I spent time on my own and figured out what I wanted. In my desperation to settle down I had attracted a relationship that was all about the settling down, but it was wrong. It was controlling, unhealthy and at points, rather scary. The universe had sent me a man who wanted to settle down, but my goodness, I was turning into a shadow of myself by being with him. Let's call him 'Mr Alarm Bells Ringing'. At this point in my life I found I wanted to give up. I was reaching the point of letting go of my ideal of what love could be. I had always promised myself I would never just settle for second best, yet here I was in a relationship with a man who was controlling me, being mean to me and keeping me small. I started smoking again (a sign for me that I was in avoidance mode) and started distancing myself from my friends who were yelling I was crazy. But before it got all too out of control my intuition kicked in: the quiet nudging voice inside me that challenged this path I was careering down. I smoked and drank to quieten the discontent inside me, but that voice came through in song words and other people's words.

The universe always has a way when it needs to get your attention. I remember one particular time sitting on my balcony overlooking the views of gorgeous Bath and listening to 'Mr Rock and Roll' by Amy Macdonald – up to this point in my life it had been one of my favourite songs of the moment, but when I listened to the words it was suddenly a prophecy of my future: 'I wish I met him, I wish I knew him before I was his bride'. In that moment I knew that if I married 'Mr Alarm Bells Ringing' I would meet, yet never marry my one true love. So I ended that relationship. I believe that that was the time I found the courage to say 'I am ready for real love'. I *was* sent a man who wanted marriage and babies and would have married me but I chose not to – I chose love and the belief that I had in love and what love really is.

I remember driving to work one day shortly after that break up and listening to Katy Perry's song 'Not like the movies' – the chorus has the words 'I know you're out there and you're looking for me, it's a crazy idea that you were made perfectly for me'. I knew in that instant of tingles going down my spine that my man, my love was on the way and I would find him eventually.

I decided to get back into acceptance mode. My life partner might not be along for years so I might as well enjoy life in the interim and so I did.

Within the month I was on a snowboarding trip with my friend. I was introduced to her boyfriend's brother and the light bulb went on. I felt drawn to him. We didn't really talk much – he was shy and so was I. I knew he was a special sort by the way he got me to use my snowboard as a toboggan down the mountain in a snow storm, whilst he rescued me. We played and had fun. It was light and silly. We started dating, him in London, me in Bath. But the universe conspires with true love and I found myself in London with work for two weeks. We dated, we laughed, we played, we connected. We made plans to move in together after six weeks, moved in at four months, and a year after our first date he whisked me off to Florence and proposed. We jumped up and down together with joy. When writing this I feel that feeling of love. I didn't think it was possible: I didn't think I'd ever be so happy in a relationship and I didn't think I could feel so completely and unconditionally loved. My 'Mr One True Love' was worth the wait, he was worth all the heartache. Every day I thank the universe that I waited and didn't jump into a relationship that felt wrong. Every day I feel blessed.

And that's what I want for you. I want you to feel that love, that unconditional, heartfelt, no holds barred, no worries love. I want to empower *you* on your journey to get there.

I used to work in marketing but now I am a full-time certified life coach. I love coaching people to reach their dreams, but especially to empower people to feel and become their best self. I know what it feels like to be single and I feel it is my mission to empower you with the skills to deal with this sometimes difficult, sometimes exhilarating, emotional, rollercoaster.

So buckle up and enjoy the ride,

love Jennifer xx

# Making this book work for you

To get the most out of this book I would recommend you take the time to do the exercises. The book starts with self-exploration and poses questions we often don't ask ourselves.

There is space in the book for you to add in your answers. The reason for this is that I have found with books that I have space to write the information in, I am more likely to take the time out to try the exercises.

If some bits are a struggle, take time out on that particular chapter to really get to grips with it.

## There are three main sections in the book:

**Creating your I-can-handle-anything foundation:** To help you work on your resilience, loving yourself, and managing your Inner Critic.

**Relying on you:** Helps you use your intuition and build your confidence.

**Date Smart:** Helps you identify what you really want and offers practical tips on how to achieve it.

This book is not a quick-fix book, but a deep look within so that you can move forward from a place of confidence, knowing who you are and what you really want.

I won't lie, some of the exercises will feel challenging to do. But I ask that you stick with them and take the time to answer the probing questions. By doing so, you'll be in the best possible place for finding the healthiest partner for you, and it will also help you love your life along the way.

# Creating your I-can-handle-anything foundation

'And suddenly you know: it's time to start something new and trust the magic of new beginnings' —Meister Eckhart

## Chapter 1

## Turning a spotlight on what's going on in your life, right now

Yes, right now as you read this book, what's going on for you? Are you out there dating, or on the sidelines hoping not to have to put yourself out there any time soon? This chapter is all about discovering more about you. We are going to gather up all the information about you so we can piece together what you're looking for and what's important to you. There are some practical exercises we will be covering and I will ask you to write things down in this book. As mentioned, to get the best out of this book, it helps to do the exercises so that you really have a solid grounding in understanding you and what is important for you.

This chapter throws you right in at the deep end and tackles some big areas such as what values are important to you and what beliefs you may have about dating. We introduce the concept of inner critic and having different parts of us wanting opposing things (sounds crazy I know), and how this inner dialogue can cause us problems without us even realising it.

It may feel like we jump into topics and then jump into

## Creating your 'I-can-handle-anything' foundation

another, but stick with it – we are creating the building blocks that help you to build the foundations of really knowing what you want, and providing a solid base to explore other topics in the book later on.

I want you to pause for a moment and think about what it is that you want to create in your life right now?

Perhaps you want to find love, or perhaps you want to just be happy and at peace with where you are right now in life.

Imagine you have a magic wand that creates the life you want. What would your life look like? What would your love life be like?

What would your future partner be like? How would they make you feel?

We will be looking more in-depth at this shortly, but for now, I want you to just write down a few notes about what it is you are looking for and what your ideal life would be like.

Imagine you have a magic wand that creates the life you want. What would your life look like?

_____
_____
_____
_____
_____
_____
_____
_____

*Turning a spotlight on what's going on in your life, right now*

What would your love life be like?

_____
_____
_____
_____
_____
_____
_____
_____
_____
_____

What would your future partner be like? How would they make you feel?

_____
_____
_____
_____
_____
_____
_____
_____
_____
_____

## Values

What's important to you? It's not a question we often ask ourselves and answer.

Values are the essence of what is important to each and every one of us. They are unique to each of us and how we live our life. Values are what we hold dear to us. So someone may find compassion or honesty really important to live by, whereas someone else may find humour or ambition really important. The thing is they are unique to each of us and there are no right and wrongs. When we know our values we can use them like a compass to guide our decisions.

Knowing our values helps us with how we date and who we date – when we follow and honour our values, life feels richer and it feels more resonant... When we don't follow our values we feel less alive and less excited with life.

To find out your values, I want you to read the sentence below and then pause, put down this book and reflect. Then I want you to write in the space below answers to the following questions:

*Think of a time or times when you felt really amazing and that life was great. Perhaps everything felt like it flowed and felt good. Some may call this a peak experience. One specific time may come to mind or it may be a few that pop into your head.*

Now I want you to answer these questions (write your answers below)

* What was going on?
* Were other people there?
* What made this time so amazing?
* If you were honouring your values in this time, what values were they?

Also reflect on:

* If money and time were no object, what would you spend your days doing?

*Turning a spotlight on what's going on in your life, right now*
..........................

_____
_____
_____
_____
_____
_____
_____
_____
_____
_____
_____
_____
_____
_____
_____
_____
_____
_____
_____
_____
_____
_____

An example of a peak experience for me was how I felt when helping a colleague with their CV. I loved being in the moment, helping them onto their path in life, helping them to move forward. I loved asking them questions that enabled them to see their experience in a different way – a way that could help them onto the career path they wanted to go on. From this, I thought about what values I was honouring – nurturing others is a huge value, being a change catalyst so instigating change in others was another value, being of service to others was important to me and helped me feel fulfilled.

Here are some values to help get you started:

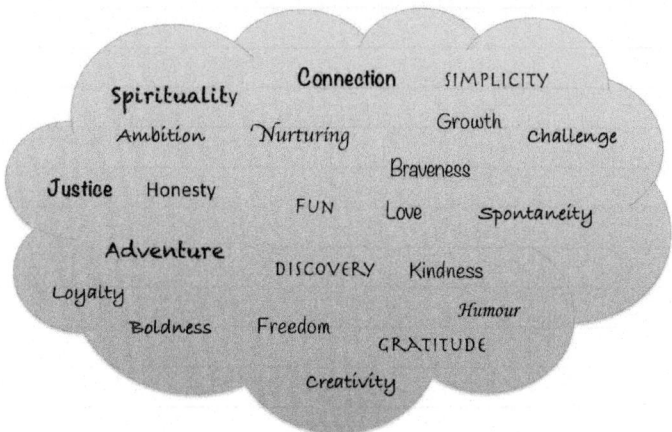

Now, think of what makes you angry or frustrated in life? Often when one of our values is being trodden on we feel frustration and anger, what would these values be for you? Was someone rude to you? What value did that affect?

_____
_____
_____
_____
_____
_____
_____
_____
_____

What values come up for you?

_____
_____
_____
_____
_____
_____
_____
_____

Sometimes values are interconnected, so you may have a value of freedom which is also linked to independence which is also linked to spontaneity. Another person may have the value of freedom and it can be completely different to what they feel independence is. All values are unique to us and often mean something different to each of us.

With any of the values that came through by doing these exercises, start with writing down a sentence or two to describe what each value means to you. This helps you connect in with your value.

An example of this for me is my value of freedom. For me, freedom is not feeling trapped, both in life and in my body. It is summed up by the visual image of running through an open field with my hands out. For me it is closely linked to independence and choice.

Next, think about prioritising your values. Which ones are most important to you in your life?

If you were to score each, ten honouring the value to the utmost and zero being not honouring it at all, what scores do you give them? So, say spontaneity is a key value to you but you are not doing much in life that is spontaneous mark it lower (e.g. 3/10).

With your top five values, what one thing could you do to put that value into action to make you more content?

_____
_____
_____
_____
_____
_____
_____
_____

Now relate how you can act on your values when you are dating? For example, if creativity is a top value but you only scored it 4/10, what could you do to increase this in the area of dating and being single? Perhaps it is going on more creative dates or perhaps it's going on dates with more creative people. Alternatively bringing more creativity through into your life with art classes, or just finding time to be creative at home (drawing, cooking, DIY etc) to allow that value to be fulfilled.

Or if you had a value of honesty, perhaps an action around this would be to be more honest with people you date about how you feel.

The table on the following page may help you set out your values and next steps.

## Turning a spotlight on what's going on in your life, right now

| Top values ranked | Description of what this value means to me | How much is this honoured out of 10? | Ways I could use this more in my life | Ways I can use this more in dating |
|---|---|---|---|---|
| 1- | | | | |
| 2- | | | | |
| 3- | | | | |
| 4- | | | | |
| 5- | | | | |

The key is when we honour our values and use them as a compass to guide us, we feel more alive, more in tune with ourselves, life feels richer and we attract people who are also feeling alive and in tune with themselves. I believe (and see regularly) we attract what we put out there.

When you are faced with a decision about dating, ask yourself, how is this in-tune with my values? How can I make a values-based decision that is right for me?

Some coaching clients have found that by bringing their values to life, by creating collages of their values and putting them where they can see them daily, helps remind them of what is important to them. What way can you remind yourself of what's important to you every day?

## Our inner world

Crazy as it sounds, I believe we all have voices within us. If we become aware and listen we notice we all have a variety of different voices inside us. Some of these voices are helpful and some are more critical or hold us back in some way.

We are all made up of lots of different parts of us: some are younger parts and some are older parts, we have bossy parts and cheerleading parts, wise parts and fearful parts. All these parts make us who we are, and all these parts want the best for us, but sometimes they can be a bit out of balance and hold us back in some way.

With dating for me, I had internal scripts about not being pretty enough, having wonky teeth, fine hair, small boobs and a big bottom – and hearing all my faults come up when I passed a mirror or prepared for a date put me in an unhelpful zone for finding love.

My inner critic would be having the dialogue like this;

'he won't like you, your chest is too small', 'how will I ever find love? I'm too much for someone to love'. My inner critic wanted to protect me from getting hurt, but it was in fact holding me back.

When we become aware of our inner world and who is leading our committee of voices, it allows us, from a place of choice, to decide if we want to listen or not listen to the voices and also to consciously decide if it is helpful to us and where we want to get to.

Pause here, take a deep breath and think about what internal voices come up for you around finding love?

In the space below, spend a few minutes reflecting on the types of messages that come up for you.

_____
_____
_____
_____
_____
_____
_____
_____
_____

How did you get on? Did you struggle to identify any voices? If you did struggle, that's completely fine. Unless we are aware of it, it can be really hard to suddenly start identifying internal voices. If you've struggled with this, I ask that over the coming few weeks, start listening to what is going on inside and what messages are coming up and when.

If you were able to identify voices, reflect for a moment on when these messages come up?

## Creating your 'I-can-handle-anything' foundation

Is it in particular situations?

_____
_____
_____
_____
_____
_____
_____

Are there any themes?

_____
_____
_____
_____
_____
_____
_____

Write all of this down.

What messages are helpful and empowering you in finding love?

_____
_____
_____
_____
_____
_____

*Turning a spotlight on what's going on in your life, right now*

_____
_____

Which messages are holding you back?

_____
_____
_____
_____
_____
_____
_____

Start to become aware of the messages, and when you hear them coming up in everyday life, ask yourself if it is helping you towards where you want to get to or holding you back.

When you are aware that you're bombarded with internal chatter and start consciously choosing whether to listen to the chatter, it shows you have the ability to choose whether to listen to the voices and thoughts inside you.

As we all have this choice, we all must be more than the thoughts and voices we hear inside us, and I believe we are. I believe we have parts of us who want to support us and protect us in some way, but can be out of balance and hold us back. Being aware of the choices you have gives you freedom to influence your inner chatter to help you move forward not hold you back. You hold the key as to when you listen to your inner voices and when you ignore them.

## Beliefs

## Turning a spotlight on what's going on inside you.

Just now, stop everything. Take a moment to focus on your breath. Breathe in for a count of four and out for a count of six. A few quiet breaths like this should make you calm and clear your thoughts and bring your focus to the present. When you are in the here and now, I want you to ask yourself 'what beliefs do I have around love?', 'what thoughts regularly pop up in my head around love?' It could be that there aren't enough men/women out there, or that there are way too many single older women than men, or that no man wants to commit? Or that all the good ones have gone so only oddballs are left. Turn a spotlight inside on what beliefs come up for you. When you have a list, ask yourself, with each one, is it true? Is it absolutely true?

Some of it may well be true – I don't know what your set of beliefs are, but what I do know is that each and every one of us, as humans, puts ourselves into a box that has certain parameters about how we believe life is. We need this otherwise we would go crazy trying to process all the information and options that comes at us daily. A part of our brain called the reticular activating system is there to find the evidence that fits with what we believe, so we unconsciously filter out all that goes against what we believe, which essentially means that our world view has a filter on it and we have a filtered view on how things are.

Every one of us has beliefs that hold us back and keep us small and when we have these beliefs out in the open, it helps us decide whether the beliefs are true or whether they are keeping us small.

When I was in my own dating slump, I had a few issues to work through. I needed to work on my self-love and acceptance (to believe I was worthy of finding love). I had a few beliefs in there as well, such as that my life would be curtailed with a husband, I wouldn't be able to be independent. I believed (at times) that men were commitment-phobes. These beliefs all held me back.

In the space below, what beliefs are holding you back?

_____
_____
_____
_____
_____
_____
_____
_____
_____

When do these beliefs come up?

_____
_____
_____
_____
_____
_____
_____

## Creating your 'I-can-handle-anything' foundation

_____
_____

What evidence can you search for to dispute any unhelpful beliefs?

_____
_____
_____
_____
_____
_____
_____
_____

What steps can you put in place to reverse these beliefs?

_____
_____
_____
_____
_____
_____
_____
_____

Hard as it may seem from the outset, we can change our beliefs by firstly being aware of them, then really looking at whether the beliefs are helpful for you and where you want to be in life. If they aren't helpful then start looking for alternative evidence to counter the belief you have. The internet can be a great place to start to find alternative belief evidence.

## Patterns we repeat

In relationships and in life, we can get caught up in certain patterns and experiences that just keep on repeating over and over again.

Looking back, I spent my twenties in a pattern of long-term relationships where I merged with my partners a bit. I took on their dreams and kind of went along for the ride. I didn't think about what I wanted and instead focused on the getting married and settling down bit. I hoped all my relationships in my twenties would end in marriage and that was my aim. The relationships were misfitted and went something like this: there would be a period of falling in love where everything was amazing and feeling 'this was the one'. Then after the honeymoon period, they would withdraw a bit as they realised I wasn't as amazing as they had built me up to be. I would crave the same adoration I initially got so would become insecure and clingy and this would send them backing off more. I would try and change myself a bit more. I would always be hoping to recapture that love they initially felt and they would never fully commit. We'd drift, me hoping that if I hung around long enough, they'd marry me. Looking back, I had some serious issues of self-acceptance and love.

Another pattern I followed later was that of a perpetual dater who had a series of first and second dates but it never

## Creating your 'I-can-handle-anything' foundation

went any further. I had gone from monogamy to serial first dater.

What patterns keep coming up when you are dating? Do you date regularly? Lose interest in people? Are you hoping to find love and settle down, but seem to come up against it?

_____
_____
_____
_____
_____
_____
_____
_____
_____

I believe that we end up experiencing certain lessons over and over again until we get that lesson and change our behaviour in some way and grow more in how we are.

If your relationship pattern was a metaphor or reminded you of an image, what would it be?

_____
_____
_____
_____
_____
_____

*Turning a spotlight on what's going on in your life, right now*

_____
_____
_____

My first metaphor would be a washing machine – going round and round on the same cycle but just with different boyfriends.

My other metaphor would be of a scary game of musical chairs where I was the only one left standing with no chair. There was definitely a scarcity of men story going on inside me at times.

What change in you would it take to break your cycle?

_____
_____
_____
_____
_____
_____
_____
_____

What do you know about yourself from that cycle? What do you need to break that cycle?

_____
_____
_____
_____

## Creating your 'I-can-handle-anything' foundation

_____
_____
_____
_____
_____

When you're aware of the patterns you follow in relationships it gives you a chance to decide consciously if you want to choose another way of being.

## Blocks

We've looked at your patterns and beliefs, we have looked at your values and what is important to you. Inside us all we have unconscious blocks that can get in the way of us finding love. This part is all around looking at what could be holding you back and keeping you in your current place. By being aware of our blocks, it helps us start working on them and looking at how they can be broken down.

In the space below, write down any benefits and good things about being single that you wouldn't have if you found love.

_____
_____
_____
_____
_____
_____
_____
_____

Turning a spotlight on what's going on in your life, right now

By finding love what does it stop you doing?

_____
_____
_____
_____
_____
_____
_____
_____

What are the benefits in being single and remaining single?

_____
_____
_____
_____
_____
_____
_____
_____

What comes up? Are you surprised by anything?

_____
_____
_____
_____
_____
_____

_____

_____

With this information, start thinking about what steps you can take to reassure the part of you with concerns in having a relationship.

For example, if you have a fear that you will get hurt, perhaps you can put in place some boundaries or limits you won't have crossed – perhaps committing to yourself to not stay with someone if that person is not willing to commit after a certain amount of time.

Awareness of the blocks that may be keeping us single help to make us conscious about why we maybe go for certain types of people, or why we may be avoiding settling down (if we are). With reflecting about what your blocks are, it gives you a chance to be aware of any self-sabotaging that may be happening when looking for love.

## You in your future relationship

We've looked briefly at inner beliefs. Lets focus on how you would like to feel in a relationship.

It's amazing how often we don't actually think about how we want to feel in a relationship, but for us to attract love we need to get on the emotional wavelength of what we want to attract (more on this later).

When we become aware of what we want and what we want to attract we can start taking steps in becoming the person we want to be in a relationship. For example, if you want to become more loving and nurturing, what ways in your life now can you do this, with or without a partner? Perhaps you could be more loving with your friends or family or yourself?

## Turning a spotlight on what's going on in your life, right now

I have found that some coaching clients who have been out of the dating game for a while really struggle with imagining themselves in a relationship, and can feel overwhelmed with knowing where to start, as it can feel such a far away place and so different from reality. If you relate to that, you're not alone. Hard as it is, try not to get overwhelmed or put off by the difference in reality, start with small manageable steps to where you want to get to.

What qualities would you want to bring out in you?

For example – your nurturing side, or fun loving part of you, or your sensual part of you.

_____
_____
_____
_____
_____
_____
_____
_____

What qualities would you want to attract?

For example, perhaps you want to find someone who is funny, or kind, or ambitious, affectionate, or sporty, to name but a few.

_____
_____
_____

*Creating your 'I-can-handle-anything' foundation*

_____
_____
_____
_____
_____

Often when we have been through lots of heartache in our lives or even if we have been hurt once, it can make us want to close ourselves off to love as it feels just too much of a risk to put yourself out there and be hurt again. I was hurt time and time again, dumped painfully (and humiliatingly a couple of times) and I thought more than once that a life on my own would be preferable to the constant pain, heartache and rejection.

If you recognise this in yourself, then the following exercise in the box below may help.

> Take a few minutes to breathe in and out and bring your focus to your body. If you allow yourself to think of the heartache and rejection you have faced in your life, where do you feel the emotional charge strongest in your body? Focus on that part and allow yourself to sink into the feeling, become aware of what's there. If the emotional charge had a colour, what colour would it be? If it had a shape, what would it be? If it had a texture, what would it be? What would it want to say to you? What does it need from you to feel love?
>
> Be aware of what comes up – uncensored – give yourself the space to sit with what comes up. If the pain moves or changes, follow it and be aware of what is then there. Emotion is energy and moves in our body and gives

> us information as to what is going on. By giving it space and listening to our bodies it gives us a chance to process experiences we've been through.

We all have places we avoid going to due to pain or fear. For example you may fear anger so avoid any confrontation. Being single can feel incredibly vulnerable and when we experience hurt it can make us want to close off that part of our lives to protect us. I completely get that desire to want to protect yourself, but I want to challenge it from a loving place. Imagine you are ninety years old and looking back over your life. Will shutting yourself off and protecting yourself from the possibility of being hurt again, have enriched or held you back in life? By closing yourself off what will you be preventing in your life? What will you be allowing? How colourful and rich will your life have been? Only you know what is right for you – but from a place of love – I want to encourage you to be open, really open, to finding love and to allow love to come in. I believe having that love helps us shine and become the person we are meant to be, and that by closing our hearts to the possibility of love it keeps us small and makes our life a duller shade of richness.

Look back over your life and specifically at relationships. I want you to imagine you are in a pick-and-mix sweet shop but instead of sweets you can choose for your bag, you can choose best bits from past relationships. Perhaps you found that humour from one boyfriend really lightened up your life, or great conversations from another boyfriend meant that you got in touch with issues that were important to you. Pick up your pen and write down what attributes you would want in your future relationship. Once you have done this, look at each attribute and quality on the list and write down what it would bring out in you and how it would make you feel. Some clients find that bringing images and pictures in can help them connect into the feeling. So for example if intimacy is something that you would feel in a relationship, how would that come through in images or sensations? Perhaps an image for intimacy would be a snuggly duvet or the feeling of silk. Whatever comes to mind for you, use it to connect into this feeling.

Some clients have trouble visualising the person they want to be with. If you find you relate to this, start small and build up. Perhaps you can imagine what it is like to hold their hand or to laugh with them or to have that person there when you come home from work. It's finding ways to start building them into your life. I used to dance to Chris Rea's 'Lets Dance' song in my kitchen and imagine I was dancing and being twirled round by my future partner. I loved putting on that song and dancing and just getting into the joy and playfulness of dance. I now dance around the kitchen with my partner, him busting out silly dance moves and me dancing with him. You too can dance your partner into reality, it's making this person start *feeling* real in whatever way you can.

## Bringing it all together

My key values are

*Turning a spotlight on what's going on in your life, right now*
..........................

Actions to bring these more into my life

Actions to bring these more into dating

Chapter four continues this journey.

## My inner world

Thoughts that come up regularly

# Creating your 'I-can-handle-anything' foundation

Some benefits I have uncovered to me remaining single are

Beliefs I have around dating

Beliefs I need to challenge

What do I want in a long-term relationship?

We will be looking in more detail at loving yourself and our inner world in chapter three.

## End of chapter summary

So in this chapter we have been looking at:

* What values are important to you
* What your ideal relationship would be
* Developing actions around the values focusing in on relationships and finding love
* Blocks and beliefs we have in finding love and come up with some actions to help us take a step forward
* Patterns we may have had in past relationships
* Internal dialogue and what is going on with it
* How to start visualising love in your life
* What you want to attract in a relationship and who you want to be in a relationship.

Now let's move onto the area of building yourself up in relationships.

## Chapter 2

## Bouncing Back

This chapter is all about building your resilience – your ability to bounce back from challenges. Dating is challenging, and putting yourself out there regularly can be even tougher. It can feel such a rollercoaster; having yet another bad date, yet another rejection or the disappointment of not liking someone and having the guilt of letting them down.

This chapter is all about building your capacity to bounce back so that the ups and downs of dating don't push you off kilter. Instead you can thrive no matter what situation you are in.

We will look at the key ways you can build your resilience so that you survive and thrive when dating and being single. Key things we will cover are: self-belief, positivity, meaning and purpose, reflecting, kindness and we will look at tools you can use to help increase your resilience.

So, let's get started!

When I was dating, I found being able to pick myself up was a much-needed skill. I found I would like someone, get excited about the possibilities and then when it all came crashing down, I would feel heartbroken and a bit lost. I didn't know why it was so difficult to find love.

No one really says it, but dating takes a lot of resilience and I want to say from the outset, I bet you have way more resilience than you think you have.

What is resilience? It's about being able to pick yourself up and bounce back when you face challenging times. It is also about being able to learn from whatever happened and move on wiser and stronger. The good thing about resilience is that we can all increase our own as it isn't something that is set in stone. Often people believe they are either resilient or not resilient, but that's a misconception – we can *all* grow our resilience.

Before we delve into specific tools, we need to get some foundations in place. This part is looking at where you are now.

## Self-belief

Believing in our own ability to do things and survive set backs is one of the building blocks for increasing resilience.

It can be surprising how much we have actually managed to get through in life when we think about it. This section is all about building up your self-belief in what is possible and what you can do, because I bet you are able to do an awful lot more than you give yourself credit for. We can all under play how awesome we are.

So now I want you in the space below to map out your love life like a graph and plot the good times and the bad times – you should end up with a graph that goes up and down several times. For each of the down times I want you to ask yourself:

What got me out of that situation? What resources did I pull on? What did I do to help myself?

## Creating your 'I-can-handle-anything' foundation

This should help you identify a list of your strengths, skills and resources to draw on when times are bad. What's this exercise all about? It's about helping you see that you have loads of things already that have helped you survive life's challenges.

Use this exercise to plot out your resilience graph; an example of this is below:

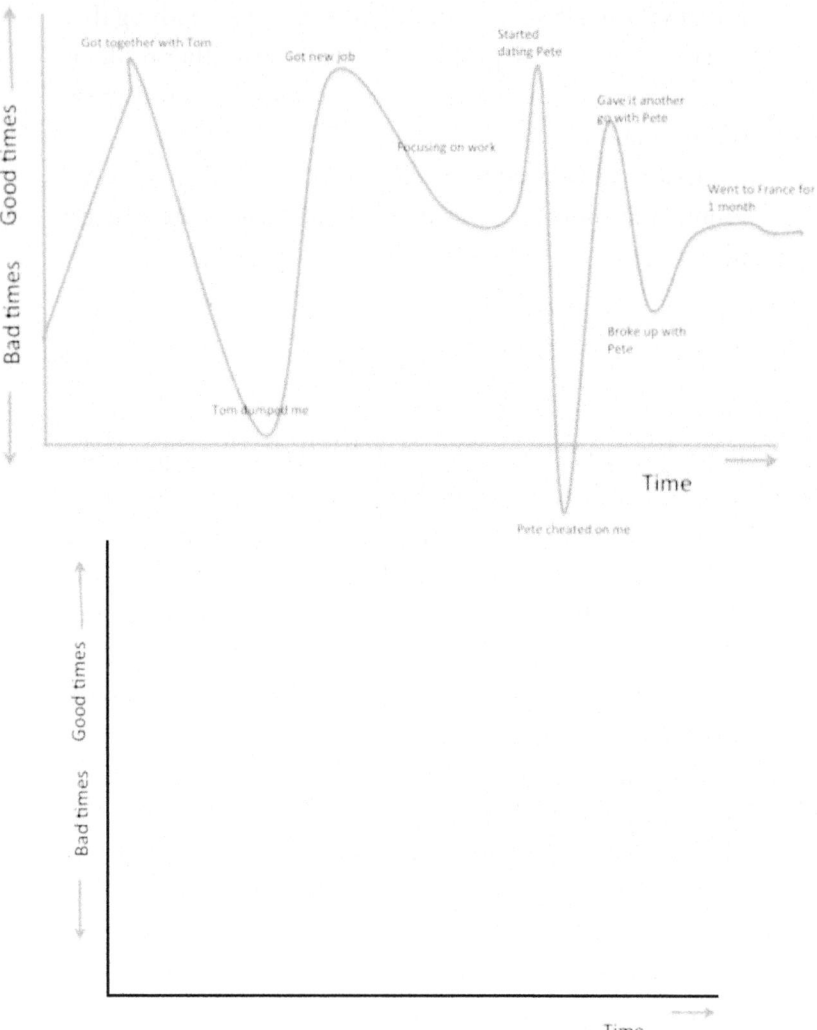

How does this relate to dating?

When were you single and when were the highs and when were the lows? What skills and strengths did you draw on within you, at each of these times? We all have strengths and skills and I bet you will be surprised at how many resources both internally and externally you can pull from when the dating world gets tough.

Take a look at your list and reflect on how much you've got through and survived so far when it comes to dating. I want you to acknowledge how you've put yourself out there despite any heartbreak you've gone through. That shows you are resilient and have it in you. We all have resilience in us and despite what you believe and what people say, we can all build up our resilience. What is needed is self-belief in you – the amazing person that you are, and in your ability at finding and attracting love.

When clients do this exercise they are often surprised at how many different skills were relied on at different stages and that the collective sum of all these skills and strengths add up to a lot. The thing is, you still have these skills and strengths – they are in you and can always be pulled from in challenging times.

I bet when you look back on it, you have got yourself through a whole load of difficult situations. Take a step back and reflect on how far you've come. Write any notes in the space below.

_____
_____
_____
_____
_____

## Creating your 'I-can-handle-anything' foundation

_____
_____
_____
_____

Now do the same for your life generally – draw the highs and the lows.




With this knowledge of the skills you have and the strengths you hold, how can this help you in your life today with dating?

_____
_____
_____
_____
_____
_____
_____

What can you draw upon?

_____

_____
_____
_____
_____
_____
_____

What can you do more of?

_____
_____
_____
_____
_____
_____

In addition to skills, it helps to have an idea of all the positive things about you, so that when you're feeling low you can help remind yourself how fab you are.

If you struggle with these exercises, ask someone you trust to help you by sharing what they see in you.

In the space below, write a list of your attributes and skills you possess that can help see you through the challenges of being single.

_____
_____
_____
_____
_____
_____

## Creating your 'I-can-handle-anything' foundation

It can help to reflect and write a list of all the compliments you have received whilst dating and from people around you. Perhaps you are really gentle and a great listener, or perhaps you are quick witted and funny. Perhaps you are kind and caring. Write down all the compliments you've received and look at the list.

_____
_____
_____
_____
_____
_____
_____

What comes up for you? If the inner chatterbox has anything to say write it down in the section in chapter one.

Add to this list by writing down all your good qualities in the space below.

_____
_____
_____
_____
_____
_____
_____

With this list, I ask that you keep it somewhere close so you can refer back to it. I pinned mine up in my kitchen when I was having a low point so I could remind myself of why I was amazing and why I would, for the right person, make an amazing partner in life.

All of the above exercises are ways to empower you, to become aware that you have loads to offer a future partner, and that as an amazing person with many strengths and attributes, you are worthy of being with an equally amazing partner. Regardless of what comes along you have the ability to weather any future dating storms that come your way.

When we believe we are capable of more, we are able to achieve more. That goes through in every area of our lives, it's tapping into the belief system in our heads and working with challenging those beliefs if they are holding us back.

Often in life, we are so forward-focused, we rarely pause and reflect to consider what strengths and parts of us we called forth to support us in challenging times. The above exercises are there to remind you of what an amazing person you are and how far you have come already. Everything in you is there waiting to be called forth and used, even things we don't see in ourselves are there but are just a bit hidden. What are the glimmers of parts of you that others see? How can you bring these forward more?

## Meaning and purpose

Often when bad things happen to us or when we face challenging times, it is easy to fall into becoming defined by that challenging event. We can get caught up in letting it define us and it becomes part of our identity. For example, if you had experienced a couple of bad break-ups where you were cheated on or lied to, it is very easy to fall into allowing that to become your story and define you. You can get into the habit of saying, 'Oh I'm always cheated on'. 'I was hurt by Alex and will now never trust anyone again'. We can all buy into the victim role and see ourselves as victims when bad things happen to us. I'm not saying if this is right or wrong, just that there are always other ways to view things that happen to us.

When we get stuck in the victim story, people see us as a victim and that then re-affirms to us that we are a victim and can't cope. This can lead to a downward spiral where we believe we aren't able to deal with the things that come our way and everyone around us also believes this. But remember we are all able to build our resilience. We are all able to choose what path we take. If nothing else in our life, we have choice: choose the hero's way…

With all the challenging events that have happened in your life, imagine you are a superhero overcoming those challenges. From the graphs of life you did earlier on in the chapter, take your most challenging time so far in your life. Ask yourself, what would a hero do in this difficult time? Being the hero or heroine of your life can change the way we look at an event. For example, a client I worked with kept being dumped after a couple of dates. When we did this exercise through the eyes of her being a hero, she saw that she was being tested for her belief in wanting to find love. With that new hero story in mind, she looked differently at the constant dumping and saw it as a chance to show she could battle through any number of bad dumping situations because as the hero of her own life, she would find love eventually.

To help you find your hero story, look back over your dating past, and think about each disaster and setback as a challenge and something to learn from or overcome. What would the lesson be that you needed to learn? What are the skills you gained? What did you learn about yourself that you wouldn't have learnt if you hadn't experienced that situation?

What meaning and purpose can you take from this situation?

_____
_____
_____
_____
_____
_____
_____

If you struggle with this, consider a person who you admire and look up to, someone who has got through lots of challenging situations and made it through. What would they have taken as the meaning from the situations you have gone through? If you really struggle with this, enlist the help of a trusted friend who can come up with the meaning behind events in your life that turns you into the hero that you are.

When we find meaning and a reason in why bad things have come our way and when we see how it has made us grow, the challenging time starts looking a bit different and it can, in a funny way, end up being a blessing in disguise.

## From a place of choice

In this section I want to talk about choice. It can feel like we have no choice and that we are stuck in certain situations. I want to share with you what I've found out about choice and how you can use it to help you become more resilient.

In every given situation we have a choice as to how we can react to whatever is going on. Often it doesn't feel like we do have a choice, and often we react automatically. Then after the situation, we wish we had reacted in a different way. With dating and being single we can be thrown into situations that test us, challenge who we are and make us feel quite alone.

We all have the internal chatterbox in our minds, but I have come to learn that we are more than just this voice and this part of us. We are more than the vocal, talkative part of us.

I have found through the daily practice of focusing on my breath, I can watch my thoughts popping into and out of my head. As I see and hear the thoughts popping into my head, I wonder if I am my thoughts, how can I observe them and see them pop in. Surely I wouldn't be able to?

Which led me to believe that there is another part of me that can observe the thoughts and feelings I feel. This part can hear the noise around me, but is able to focus on what it wants to focus on – so it can focus on my thoughts I'm having or can focus on the music from the radio etc. When I am in this space of listening and watching my thoughts but not becoming attached to them and disappearing off onto another train of thought, I can choose what thoughts I want to pay attention to. This is part of what mindfulness is all about – bringing awareness to right now, being aware of the thoughts and feelings we have but just observing not reacting to those thoughts and feelings.

When I choose what thoughts I want to pay attention to, I have found that this gives me choice.

By regularly practicing focusing on my breath I have found that it enables me to take a step back and not react straight away when I am in certain situations; it has given me space in my head. This has meant that when I am put in challenging situations, I have had a tiny bit more space to pause and decide how I want to react instead of reacting straight away. I may still choose to react how I automatically would have, but it is from a place of choice rather than a place of reactivity. So I am more empowered to make choices in my life.

So how on earth does this relate to resilience and bouncing back? When you are going through a challenging time, it is very easy to get swept up in the emotional rollercoaster. It can feel like we are having something done to us, rather than being able to do anything. In each moment though, you have a choice. Maybe not a choice of what is happening to you, but a choice about how you react to what is going on. We can choose to get swept up or we can choose to stand strong and like a tree sway in the breeze of life. And when you are in the midst of a difficult time using your breath to anchor you in the moment is a great way to connect you back into the space of choice. Victor Frankl's book *In Search Of Meaning* spoke of this choice we all have – no matter what happens no one can take away that freedom from us, and it is our choice to decide how we want to use it.

This exercise is called 'Leaves on a Stream' and helps unhook you from your thoughts.

---

### Leaves on a Stream

* Find a comfortable position, sitting or lying and either close your eyes or fix them on a spot
* Imagine a gently flowing stream
* Imagine there are leaves floating on the surface of the water
* For the next five minutes take every thought that pops into your head (whether it's a picture or a word) and put it on top of a leaf and let it float down the stream

## Creating your 'I-can-handle-anything' foundation

- Do this with every thought – happy, sad, etc.
- This exercise is about unhooking ourselves from thoughts, so put all thoughts on the leaves
- Don't aim to get rid of thoughts, just step back from them and observe them
- If your thoughts stop, watch the stream until the thoughts start again
- If your mind says 'this is silly', 'it's too hard' put those thoughts on a leaf too
- If you think you're not doing it properly, simply pause and restart the exercise with that thought on a leaf
- If you find you get fused to a thought and start thinking about something, such as what needs doing later, just bring yourself back to the start of the exercise kindly and start again.

When we know we can choose how we react in a given moment and how we react to situations in our life, we can then choose the mindset we adopt.

Research shows that there are two types of mindset we can adopt – a growth mindset and a fixed mindset. A growth mindset sees challenges as opportunities to grow and evolve, that things can change and that it is within our power to change. A fixed mindset sees things as being more permanent and that you are given a particular set of skills and can't change. This fixed mindset has more of a pessimistic take on life situations, a person who adopts this mindset sees things as happening to them and not being able to do anything about it. The good news is that if you see yourself identifying with the fixed mindset you can change this. We can all learn to develop a growth mindset, seeing life and the challenges we come up against as an opportunity to learn and grow.

So how do you change your mindset? A way of doing this involves becoming aware of knowing what mindset you fall into and catching yourself when being pessimistic about a situation. It's stopping yourself and thinking of all the good things going on and how you can learn from the situation. And by the knowledge that we can grow and change and aren't fixed in our ability to do anything.

## Emotions

When we are going through tough times we often find lots of emotions come up for us. The next section is about how positive emotions can help us in our challenging times.

## Positivity

Another rather surprising aspect of resilience is positivity. Research shows when we bring in more positive experiences in our life, we thrive and have an increased resilience bank so that when tough times come along, we are more able to manage them and bounce back.

Let's bring on the positivity!

Injecting moments of positivity into your day keeps you open to more positive things coming. From reading around the laws of attraction, there are some key things I have discovered. We are all made up of energy, every single cell when drilled down in our body is made up of energy and we vibrate at certain frequencies. When we are feeling completely happy and experience the feeling of joy (or any other positive emotion), when we bring more positive emotion into our days, a funny thing happens –

more positives come our way. The opposite also can occur for negative emotions. We have all experienced a really great day – the sun shines through the window, you wake up before your alarm, everything goes well, from the short trouble-free commute to the day of everything flowing effortlessly. This isn't a coincidence. When we start the day with positive feelings we put out what we want to receive. We get a vibrational match and life feels great. There are ways we can bring more of this positive emotion into our everyday life, and by injecting our day with moments of exquisiteness we increase our feelings of happiness. Off the back of this, things flow to us and opportunities come along. So this section is about bringing more positive emotion into your day and your life so it feels great and you have a bank of resilience to call on when times take a down turn.

---

Positivity Exercise to try:

Have a think and reflect on your day. Write out a standard day and then go through it, thinking about how you can make it more positive and filled with positive emotion.

Here are some ideas to get you started:

* Set the alarm slightly earlier so you have a more peaceful, chilled start to the day
* Take the scenic route to work that takes a bit longer but passes through a gorgeous park
* Have your favourite flowers, postcard or photo on your desk at work reminding you of good times
* Make time for friends who make you feel full of joy and fun and avoid friends who don't
* Make a batch of your favourite meal and keep it in the freezer so you always have something yummy to

> heat up in the evening after work
> * Do something creative that you love.

Research by Barbara Fredrickson, a positive psychologist guru, has found that creating positive emotions (joy, amusement, awe, love, serenity, interest, inspiration, hope) portfolios really help. This involves compiling a scrapbook full of whatever ways to generate that emotion. I recently created an amusement document on the computer with links to my favourite funny clips from the TV, plus jokes and funny stories that always make me giggle. This gives me something to look at when I need an amusement boost.

Whatever ways you can think of, start compiling a list of what could bring more joy into your life.

At my last stressful office job, I took time out to get my favourite coffee, I brought in a plant and flowers for my desk and made sure I scheduled in a few lunch time runs a week to enable me to feel great despite what was going on in the day. And yes, it was sometimes hard to get up and go for a run when everyone was working miserably through lunch, but I had to remind myself that it was their choice and my choice was for health, aliveness and joy in my life.

Positivity gets a bad wrap with some people believing that it's not keeping it real. I disagree. We can keep it real and also bring joy into our days. This goes for loving ourselves as well – I have dedicated a whole chapter to this as I believe it is key for finding love.

## Self-belief

Self-belief can be a bit of a tricky one with dating and being single. It can feel like it's impossible to build up your self-belief, especially if you have had one too many bad dates, or just find that you actually aren't even going on dates. Well, now is the time to change that!

Do you believe you will find love? Do you believe you are loveable and that there is someone out there for you?

I hope the answer is a resounding yes, but for those of you who aren't so sure, (and I would like to say I was in that not-so-sure camp) read on. I know I really struggled with this one, and reading back over old journals I was surprised at how much I questioned ever finding love.

I went through stages (after too many bad dates) of not being sure what I could bring to a relationship. At this point my inner leader spoke up to challenge this. I started collating nice things people said about me. I started focusing on what I could bring to a loving relationship and I started looking for examples of people who found love later in life and were blissfully happy. I started changing my beliefs bit by bit. I didn't want to listen to the scaremongering around me from the media saying I had left it too late and that there were way too many women to men in my age bracket. I made a choice to seek out examples of people finding true love and not just settling. I found (when I looked) that there were lots of examples, like my friend who found love and didn't settle, or Cat Deeley who found love and married at thirty-six.

What are your beliefs around love and finding the one?

I want you to pause for a minute and just reflect on what you believe. What beliefs around love are holding you back?

_____
_____
_____
_____

_____
_____
_____
_____

Take a few moments to write down the script of the life you are buying into.

_____
_____
_____
_____
_____
_____
_____
_____

If I'd have done this, mine would have gone something like this: I won't find anyone, everyone settles down, everyone pities me, I am alone and I can't have children as it's too late. Then I get bitter and twisted and everyone hates me – oh and I'd die alone! Dramatic I know but it is amazing how the fearful part of us over exaggerates and soon enough it becomes a self-fulfilling prophecy.

So this script you've written, I want you to put it to one side and write a new script for love, one based on optimism and hope.

This new script is one that has you finding love and finding it at the right time for you. Write about all the parts of you that your new partner will love, all the fun things you'll do together and all the life enhancing things this

### Creating your 'I-can-handle-anything' foundation

will bring to you. I want you to feel this as if it has already happened, allow it to start as a flutter in your stomach or a fizzing and grow so it goes into every cell of your body.

_____
_____
_____
_____
_____
_____
_____
_____
_____

What are your beliefs about handling life regardless of what comes your way? Do you see yourself as strong? Unable to cope? Or perhaps somewhere in the middle?

I believe we are only sent the challenges we can handle, and this leads me onto another important part of resilience – having meaning and purpose around things that happen. So when you look back over your love life and life to date, what story are you telling yourself and others? Is it one of being a victim and having things happen to you, or is it one of being a hero and learning lessons from your experiences?

## Resilience tools

## Kindness

Research shows that by practicing acts of kindness in our lives it makes us feel happier and we can use it as a tool to increase our resilience. Look for ways every week to practice kind acts. Perhaps it is buying a cup of tea for a homeless person, letting someone have your seat on the train, sending a present to someone in the post, letting someone in when you're driving or in the queue at the post office. The key to practicing acts of kindness is that we mix it up and don't make it another thing to add to our to-do list. We may commit to doing five random acts of kindness one day and then nine over the course of the week after. Variety is the spice of life and it is the key for getting the most out of this tool. Also something I have found is not to tell everyone about your kind acts – keep them to yourself, knowing that you are kind at your soul. This in itself can really help our self-esteem as we view ourselves in a different way when being kind.

Before I move on from kindness, there is also something in being kind to ourselves and showing compassion to ourselves. When we are going through tough times, sometimes our inner critic comes up letting us know about all the things we have failed at and all the things we could have done better, which makes us feel even worse. This is the time to show yourself kindness. In the next chapter, we will look in more detail about how we can show kindness to ourselves.

## Gratitude

When we are going through challenging times, being grateful for what we have is often the last thing on our mind. Research shows when we are grateful and practice gratitude for what is good in our life, it helps get us on the upward spiral and gets us to look for the good and not the bad in situations. Gratitude doesn't need to be for the big things in life – it can be being grateful for things such as getting to see a gorgeous tree or flowers on the way to work, or there not being a queue at the coffee shop in the morning, or sharing a joke with a work colleague. Whatever the things you can find to be grateful about, try to write three of them in a notebook at the end of each day. This practice can improve your mood and make you aware of the positives in your life.

## Support network

Having a strong support network of friends and family around us is shown to be a key component in building our resilience. So who is in your support network? What ways can you connect with your friends and family to ensure you have a ready-primed group to support you when you hit challenging times? Having one or two people you can call at any time of day can be really helpful especially when you are going through a particularly challenging time.

Also look back over all the things you learnt about yourself in the graph of life exercise. What other ways can you build a support network around you?

## Music

I am a massive fan of using music to help through situations. It helps me express who I am. Set about creating a playlist for when you feel down to lift you up.

Create a 'find love' playlist that reminds you of what the whole purpose is of you putting yourself out there again and again.

Create a 'sad songs' playlist for when you need a good cry to get it all out your system. (A word of caution though on the 'sad songs' playlist: make it an infrequent playlist to call on, not a regularly-played one as it could sink you further into sadness and misery). When I was dating I created a 'bouncing back' playlist with songs such as 'Chumbawamba' – Tubthumping (I get knocked down).

## Humour

Finding the humour in situations is a great way of lightening the challenge you are going through and laughter is a great stress reliever, so now is the time for finding the TV shows that make you laugh, hanging out with the friends who make you giggle and looking for the funny side of situations.

In this chapter we have looked at self-belief and growing yours to show you've been through a lot already and have many skills and strengths to help you face the challenges of dating.

We have looked at our inner experience, blocks and beliefs that hold us back. We looked at tools to help bring more resilience into your life.

I hope this chapter has helped you know there are many ways you can grow your resilience and there is always hope for the future.

## Chapter 3

## Let's start with loving you

When we are looking for love, it can be really hard to love and be kind to ourselves. Loads of internal worries can come up, and when we don't have a special someone there to give us love and make us feel good, we can feel like we are lurching from one thing to another, feeling completely unlovable, unlikeable and wanting to shrink and hide.

This chapter is all about loving the amazing person that you are, so that you love yourself and send out 'I am worthy', 'I am lovable' vibes no matter what is going on with your love life.

When we are dating or single, one of the big things about not being in a relationship is not feeling loved by someone special. Often we forget to fill up our own 'love reservoir', or don't know how to fill it up. We can feel low in ourselves and in a bid to fill that void, we keep busy, drink too much, have one-night stands, and stay in relationships that make us feel even worse just to be with someone. We can end up doing even more of the things that aren't helping us in a bid to fill the silence of being at home and on our own.

### Let's start with loving you

But I want more for you, and this chapter is all about giving you some other ways to get more for you, regardless of whether you are in a relationship or not, and to keep your love tank full.

So to start with, let's reflect on what's going on for you:

How easy do you find it to be loving towards yourself?

_____
_____
_____
_____

What ways do you look after and pamper yourself?

_____
_____
_____
_____

If you were to turn a spotlight on what your internal chatterbox says to you, how do you talk to yourself? Are there words of love or criticism?

_____
_____
_____
_____

Where do you fit on your list of priorities?

_____
_____

My own journey with loving myself has been a journey I have needed to go through to really be in a place to find a healthy love. I knew I was ok at pampering myself and looking out for me (most of the time), but accepting and really truly loving myself was a challenge and one where I bounced from one end of the scale to the other.

So let's start.

## What my internal inner critic says to me:

I mentioned this already in the previous chapters – by seeing that we are made of lots of different parts we can have more awareness of who is in charge of our inner world. We can start recognising certain voices that come up at certain times, and we can choose if we want to listen to that voice or whether we want to listen to a more helpful loving part of us.

As said before, crazy as it sounds, we all have inner voices in our heads. Some are helpful inner voices and some are not so helpful. These can sound like a constant commentary on life going by, an internal chatterbox that has an opinion on the right and wrong way to do things. These internal voices all have the overall goal of keeping us safe in some way, shape or form, but they can get a bit out of balance. When they get out of balance they can exaggerate how things are and make us feel worse. They make us feel like there actually is more to be scared of than there really is.

For me I always had a grumpy, pessimistic voice and another, supportive cheerleader voice inside me. These voices gave me opposing views on life and it got a bit loud – and confusing at points knowing what to listen to. I want you for now to just become aware of the voices, especially the negative voices going on inside you. When you become aware of your inner voices, it gives you a chance to choose whether to listen to them. When we aren't aware we just become 'fused' to the voices and think that the voice we hear is the absolute truth that we often don't stop to question. It's like having an internal radio. We have a choice of what channel we have it tuned to, the channel can be supportive or negative to us. To be clear, that voice can and will show up regardless, but it's whether we pay attention to it or not – and this is what I want to spend time on now.

To help become aware of what our internal chatterboxes are saying, spend time in quiet and practise focusing on your breath. This gives a great chance to see what thoughts and feelings you have coming up. Specifically, look back over the answers you gave at the start of the chapter (page 54). If you were turning the spotlight to what was going on internally when you thought about and then wrote down the answers, what came up?

There is an exercise on focusing on breath and being aware of what comes up on page 43.

Often some inner voices come up more strongly when we are in certain situations, such as when we're getting ready for a date, or going out somewhere new.

When you become aware of the different voices, some may be high pitched, some may be calmer, bring your attention to what goes on in your body with the voices. Start to become aware of the body posture you get in when you are listening to the unsupportive inner voice. Is your posture hunched and small? Is it tight and squashed? Whatever it is, I want you to listen to the voice of your chatterbox and then take a breath in and get your body into the complete opposite pose. What does that look like for you? Is it standing up straight? Is it sitting leaning back and relaxed? How is your breath? When you find you have an inner-critic attack, practise getting into the complete opposite body posture. It's a way of using your body to get out of the mindset of the part that's keeping you small. Commit this new posture to your memory so that you can come back to it whenever you feel yourself getting an inner-chatterbox attack.

Another way to handle inner messages that come up is to ask yourself: 'Is it true?' 'What happens to my energy when I hear this inner voice?' 'Do I curl up or do I grow and expand?' If this voice looked like something and had a name other than yours what would it be? Is it helping you with where you want to get to in your life?

Add that name and a picture here:

Within all of us, amongst all these voices, there is a wise inner leader. This part of us wants the best for us and knows what is the right path for us. Within the bonus materials, there is a visualisation to connect with this wise part of you and when connected, it is a helpful resource to rely on and is there to support you in your journey in life.

When we recognise what internal parts are in charge

and we are aware of our inner critic/sabateurs, it gives us a chance to decide if we want to listen and believe what we are being told, or if we want to believe something else that potentially is more helpful to us.

Bringing awareness to our inner world is the first step in making changes, as we can start to choose what inner messages are supporting or holding you back.

We are now going to look at decluttering.

## Decluttering

I believe that having a safe haven you can retreat to that is just for you creates a strong foundation and enables you to fully put yourself out in the world, knowing there is always a safe space to return to. So, does your living space give you that haven and space for a strong foundation? Great if it does, but often we overlook the importance of creating a safe haven.

Ask yourself: 'What is your home like?' Are you living and enduring, waiting in the hope for a special someone to come along and enable you to move out of your current home? If so, then I want to give you some tough love. Our home is the place we can escape from the world and feel safe and comfortable. When we are living somewhere we don't like, don't feel safe in, is dirty, messy, cluttered and not how we'd like it, it first of all makes us feel rubbish and we don't want to spend time there. It also doesn't give us the sanctuary we all need from life and the dating world and it is a massive energy drainer. I am a massive advocate (as you can probably gather) that having a home that is a delight to come back to is, I believe, key to having a strong foundation and feeling grounded. If things aren't feeling right, yet you are putting up with it and accepting it in the hope that someone will come along and you can move out, it doesn't give you the message you're worth it, which you *so* are. Now is the time to create the place you love.

It doesn't need to be costly to turn a house into a haven. It takes a few simple things such as getting rid of the clutter and the broken things, perhaps it's giving it a lick of paint or changing a duvet cover, getting a new rug for the floor. Perhaps it's giving your place a spring clean. These things all help in making it a place to retreat and feel safe in.

Decluttering our possessions is a way to get rid of what is not serving us well. This process also gives us a chance for a declutter emotionally. Most of us have a tendency to hold onto physical things. Perhaps they remind you of a time in your life, or even though you're not keen on something you feel bad about getting rid of it. The thing is, holding onto physical things can make us feel bad and takes a bit of our energy away, it means we need to find space for all the stuff and that means we often need more room because of it. I am from a family of hoarders so I know I have struggled at times to reduce down my belongings. I used to dread moving house, as did my family who used to help me! When I started decluttering, I started feeling lighter and liberated. The reason why I am writing about decluttering in this chapter on self-love is that decluttering our possessions helps with the emotional decluttering. This all helps with growing your love for yourself by removing the blocks and baggage both physically and emotionally.

Tackle a room or area at a time and once you've been round all the rooms, start again, as you can always clear more. Ask yourself – 'have I used it in the last six months?' If you haven't then get rid of it as the likelihood is that you won't. Also ask yourself – 'What things do I have that make me feel bad, or have an negative emotional connection?'

## Let's start with loving you

Perhaps you still have gifts or cards from an ex that treated you badly, or have a stack of unwanted presents that you know deep down you don't like and won't use. This is the time to bag them up and give them to charity so that someone else can get use out of it. (This can serve as one of your random acts of kindness).

Once you've decluttered, have a think about what you want your home to feel like. Do you want it to be a calm haven? Do you want a sensual passion-filled room? A room to fuel creativity to flourish? Then Google ideas of how that would look and create that room through a vision mood board.

After creating your haven and a space you love, set about having a space that is ready for your partner. Crazy as it sounds, when I was single, I used to have a spare drawer ready and waiting for my life partner to use. For me, this was my way of creating space in my home and was a sign to the universe to say, I'm ready for him! Bring it on!

Cleansing your home of negative energy and staleness is a great way to start afresh as well – there are books dedicated to this. Some of the ways to cleanse a room include using sage sticks (can be bought on Amazon), salt in the corner of rooms and using a humming bowl to create sound that shakes up the energy in your home.

Now we've decluttered your living space, it's time to look at what is going on internally.

## Forgiveness

We all carry around baggage from previous relationships and previous experiences. As well as decluttering our external surroundings, it is important to declutter our inner world

## Creating your 'I-can-handle-anything' foundation

too. Practising forgiveness is one way to declutter some of the internal baggage we carry around and I have been amazed at the benefits of this in my own life. In life, we all get hurt and hold grudges and resentments towards people who have hurt us, especially when it comes to love. When we hold onto these resentments and hurts, they keep a bit of us held in a place that keeps us closed from new experiences and new love. I know I had my heart broken several times, and had some pretty horrible experiences with a couple of my long-term exes that really made me angry and closed off to love. I would relive and go over the hurts in my head and come up with all manner of come-backs I would say if I could. I would imagine revenging my exes by looking lovely and not being available for them any more. But this all held me back. It closed me off and took up a lot of my energy. I want to save you the heartache and pain that I went through in not letting go.

The thing with forgiveness is it's not condoning or accepting the behaviour or hurts we have experienced against us. By forgiving, we are not letting *them* off the hook – instead we are letting *ourselves* off the hook by not keeping part of our vital life force held in a past event, tied up in the toxicity of resentment. This is all about the process of reducing the emotional charge of each of the past hurts you feel. Research indicates when we do this we feel happier in ourselves.

A great exercise from the book *Lucky Bitch* by Denise Duffield-Thomas is;

Start with writing a list of all the people you hold resentments against, especially with love.

I was surprised when I did this just how much resentment I had inside me for people that I hadn't seen or been hurt by for years, although I didn't feel I held resentments.

Next go through the list one by one and say, 'I forgive you I'm sorry and I love you,' I also add in the additional

## Let's start with loving you

line, 'I'm letting this go.' And sometimes I visualise a balloon being released.

Another brilliant tool to help with forgiving the 'hard to forgive' acts is to use EFT (Emotional Freedom Technique). This is all about tapping on the various energy meridians and repeating key phrases around forgiveness. There are great resources on YouTube where you can follow the person and tap along repeating the phrases out loud. I was quite skeptical about EFT initially, but wow, I find it a brilliant way to reset my internal circuits. To find out more go to YouTube and search 'EFT for Forgiveness.' Brad Yates does some brilliant videos on EFT.

Finding meaning and purpose and some benefit in the hurts we've experienced is another way of reducing the emotional charge on hurts from the past. It sounds counterintuitive with some hurts, but I ask you give it a try. I had one particular ex who I dated for a couple of years and travelled round the world with. We had a particularly brutal break up and he did and said things that were hurtful. At the time I felt so destroyed, but I can now look back and see that even though he still said and acted in a hurtful way, he actually opened my life up in new directions. He taught me to snowboard and he opened my eyes to a different kind of living, one that was in flow. I found meaning in how it was, looking from his eyes. I can now see that he was unhappy in himself and reacted badly. This doesn't mean I want to hang out and be friends with him, just that I am willing to forgive him, let go and move on.

We're all made up of good and bad and we all do things that we regret – that is being human. We have a choice though and I want for you to choose the path that allows and opens up new life for you, new experiences and love. Being able to love completely means letting go, with love, the hurts against us so that we can love fully in the future. Staying on the topic of forgiveness, self-forgiveness is another massive area that can hold us back. We need love and compassion for ourselves, as we are on a journey and we all make mistakes along the way.

Perhaps you hurt someone a long time ago and you feel bad that you behaved the way you did. Perhaps you resent parts of your body (big nose, chunky thighs, pale complexion) for holding you back? Whatever the resentment is about, remember the incident and send love to it and say 'I forgive you'. It does make a difference doing this, believe me.

Forgiveness is a process, one that takes time, but it is really worth doing as it gets rid of the old, in preparation for the exciting new that will be coming into your life.

## Self-Acceptance

We've worked on decluttering and forgiveness, the next step in this chapter is self-acceptance. This is all about accepting ourselves, as we are, right now without changing anything – big bottom, small boobs, freckles and all. It's about accepting and loving ourselves inside and out regardless of the external validation we are receiving from others. This can be a tricky one to figure out as we are built from an early age to compare ourselves to others and conditioned to listen to authority figures around us for approval in how we behave. Add into that all the unrealistic (and photoshopped) images in the media and around us – it can't help but make us feel like we just don't hit the mark in how we are.

When we are single, it can be easier said than done

## Let's start with loving you

to feel acceptance, especially as we are in a society that looks at fixing problems. A single person is often seen as a 'problem' that needs fixing. This can have the knock-on effect of making you feel like you don't belong, aren't good enough, are a fraud, aren't pretty enough, tall enough, smart enough, kind enough. This has the effect of us accepting less – we feel we don't deserve any more. We can get into the mindset that we are lucky to get any attention from anybody as we are so unlovable and unacceptable. This simply isn't true.

When I was dating, I had some massive discrepancies, feeling attractive at times and then incredibly unattractive and unlovable at other times. My teeth had train-track braces with dental elastics to boot, my hair was thinner than I wanted and my breasts were a disappointing A cup not the C cup I wanted (and believed every man in the world wanted as well). These were all major points of worry and vulnerability. I was very good at remembering all the put downs I had received from past boyfriends, but remembering the lovely compliments were a lot harder to pull to mind.

So I started the process of self-acceptance – slowly.

For each part of me I was unhappy with, I made a point of looking for the benefits. So for the benefits in having small breasts, I could wear pretty dainty tops without the need for a big bra.

I looked at the benefits of having braces. It gave me time out from dating, it meant that men who were only interested in my looks were quickly whittled out. It meant that I got the straight teeth I had always dreamed of. And for me it was a massive commitment to myself to put me first instead of putting a man first and putting a man's preferences on how I looked first as well. I also wanted to change my belief that these parts of me were deemed ugly and unacceptable by others. I looked for women in the public eye who had accepted who they were and were still beautiful. For my breasts, I Googled women who were smaller busted and started collating a list of women who were accepting of themselves as they were with small breasts and not an implant in sight.

So in the space below or in your journal, write down the body parts you are unhappy with. What do you not like about them? What are the benefits of these body parts? Perhaps you have always hated your bottom or your thighs but actually looking at them through the lens of an appreciator they are womanly and curvaceous.

_____
_____
_____
_____
_____
_____
_____
_____

Who in the public eye has similar body parts and is deemed as beautiful? Create a list of those who are beautiful regardless of what society deems as an imperfection.

With each body part, what are the benefits of them being the way they are?

_____
_____
_____

### Let's start with loving you

_____
_____
_____
_____
_____

I found that having small breasts meant that I didn't need to worry about a bra if I didn't want to wear one. It also meant that I was less likely to jump into bed with someone as I was uncomfortable being vulnerable, which meant that it was a good way to make sure I was comfortable with a person first. My hair meant I developed compassion for those around me – I suddenly saw that we all have things we are sensitive about. Mine was my thin hair. So instead of looking at people who maybe had something that is deemed as 'not normal' by society, I would instead send love and compassion their way. It made me realise that we are all on our own journey in life and all have doubts and insecurities.

Creating a list of the things I was happy about within myself also helped.

My list looked something like this:

* Nice smile
* Striking eye colour
* Soft skin
* Lovely waist and flat stomach
* Nice legs
* Nice colour hair.

In the space below, write down your own list of things you are happy with about yourself:

## Creating your 'I-can-handle-anything' foundation

_____
_____
_____
_____
_____
_____
_____
_____
_____
_____
_____
_____
_____

Next I pinned this list to the wall so that every time I felt down and unattractive, I could remember the things that were lovely about me.

I also went through emails and messages I had received from friends and exes that complimented me and compiled a list so that I could see that actually I had lots of very lovable bits and that others felt the same.

And we all have things we are complimented on. Sometimes we filter these out, but maybe ask a close friend or family member you trust what they love about you. When you hear what others say, try not to dismiss it straight away but instead, breathe in, thank the person and then say nothing else.

Next I started on the internal messaging – I had confidence in some areas of my life, but definitely felt I was unlovable. My internal chatterbox went something like this: 'your hair is too thin', 'you're not funny enough', 'you're

## Let's start with loving you

not interesting enough', 'your bottom is too big', 'you're not adventurous', 'you're too much', 'you're too clingy', 'I will never find someone who wants to be with me'.

All this was swirling around in my head emitting out a completely unlovable vibe and a 'I'm not good enough for anyone' vibe. And I wondered why I was attracting men that treated me that way!

So what changed? How did I end up attracting my loving, caring partner? I worked on me and my self-love. I did this by exploring my inner voices in my head and challenging the messages I was giving myself. We will work through these exercises below so that you too can challenge what is holding you back and keeping you stuck and from growing into your full potential.

## Let's look at your self-love

It's funny how internally we are very able to keep a pretty long list of all the put-downs we have received, but bringing to mind a positive one is tricky. I found that the energy I was putting out with dating was giving that vibe as well. I set about looking at how I could make the most of what I had, and love and accept me as I am. I wrote lists about what I loved about me, I sent love to the parts I was struggling with and I found benefits in them being the way they were.

I hated my fine hair, so I set about seeing a trichologist and got a hair cut that made it look nicer. I also started appreciating the curliness, softness and colour of my hair. I bought pretty hair clips and tried styles that took away from the fineness of my hair – and then I found I started getting compliments about how lovely my hair was pinned up, and that was a turnaround.

## Creating your 'I-can-handle-anything' foundation

Now I want you to look at *your* list of things you don't like about your body, and for each one, find something you love about them and focus on that. When we focus and bring our attention to something we don't want we get more of it. This I know happens time and time again with my hair. Whenever I focus and worry it is getting thinner and more of my scalp is showing, well you guessed it, it becomes thinner. I then worry more and my favourite inner-worrier voice – Scary Mary – pops her head up with the doom and gloom that my hair will all fall out, I will be completely unattractive and never find love. Oh, and will die alone and bitter. All this has come from the focus being on a worry that my hair was getting thinner, a complete snowball. But when I focused on the things I loved about my hair, the colour, the softness, the curliness, I felt more love and less hate for it and this I'm sure, helped my overall mood and health, and surprise surprise suddenly it stopped falling out.

I urge you to spend time sending love to each of the parts you don't like. Focus on the things you do love about them and forgive them for not being exactly as you want them to be.

Forgiving ourselves and parts of ourselves sets free the balls of resentment through our bodies, so that all our energy can be freely flowing through our bodies and not stuck.

Try this: practise Loving Kindness Meditation, take a look at my bonus materials to download your free version. It can really help change how we view ourselves and others so we feel more love and compassion.

Remember on page 16 we looked at beliefs? Next I want you to get that list of beliefs you have about yourself and life, and I want you to write some new sayings and affirmations to fill your day and your head.

Some affirmations and sayings I have found helpful and I love to use are:

* Hip hip hooray there is joy in every day (Louise Hay)
* I love me
* I am ready for love and I am ready now
* I love me – I love all of me
* I am lovable
* I am love
* I am complete
* I am whole and lovable.

Space for affirmations:

Another idea is using afformations – these are different to affirmations as they are all about asking ourselves a question:
* Why do I attract such amazing life partners?
* Why am I so lovable?

It tricks our brain into looking for reasons why we are the statement we have affirmed. For more on this check out *Book of Afformations*, by Noah St. John.

## Your love reservoir

Years ago I was introduced to the book *Five Languages of Love* by Gary Chapman, and even though it was designed for couples in relationships, it helped me figure out how I could make myself feel more loved. If you haven't read the book, there are five different languages – Acts of service, Physical touch, Time, Gifts, Words of affirmation.

You can find out about your language of love on the website www.5lovelanguages.com. How did this help me? It meant that I knew what I needed to do to keep my love tank full. It gave me more information about what was important for me so that I could still feel love, regardless of whether I was in a relationship or not.

I believe that when I started putting myself first and making sure my love tank was full and looking after myself, this all made me feel I was lovable and deserved to be treated well. For me, that involved making time on my own as enjoyable and kind to myself as possible.

My languages of love were physical touch and time. So I knew that I needed to find ways to ensure I wasn't missing out. For physical touch, I booked in regular massages, I got myself a hot water bottle and super snuggly duvet and pillows so I could snuggle up and feel great. Time was also important to me, so I booked in quality time with myself, creating a list of all the things I loved to do, and doing them.

When you have your language of love, what ways can you bring this more into your life to keep your love tank full? Perhaps you feel loved when you have words of affirmation. How can you let yourself know how much you love you?

## Creating a pampering day of kindness and love for you:

Pampering yourself and making yourself feel good are things that can fall down the list of priorities when you don't have someone around. I noticed I missed the affection – someone making a fuss of me, someone letting me know I was loved. Yes, I had friends but I felt it wasn't the same as having someone to snuggle up to and feel looked after. I started realising that if I didn't start pampering myself, no one else was going to. There was no one currently on the horizon who was going to pamper me, so I was missing out on all the love and kindness and pampering I would get from a partner. So I set about making the time on my own as enjoyable as possible, rather than a prison sentence to be endured, waiting for that someone to do it for me. By doing this, positive things happened. I started really looking forward to time on my own and I cherished the treats I had lined up for myself. I also became more comfortable with my own company and found when I filled up my love tank, I had more love for others. This was a massive lesson to me. I was brought up by my mum who put everyone first, but I knew when I did this myself I felt resentful and snappy – things were done but not from a place of love. Instead they were from a place of endurance, of resentment and then of guilt for doing something nice but not being able to do it without feeling resentful. When I felt pampered, loved and had given myself time to do the things I wanted, I found I had more love (genuine love, time and kindness) to share with others – I wanted to help others. So the lesson for me was that instead of being a martyr, it was important for me to see that my needs were also important – irrespective of whether I was in a relationship or not.

## Creating your 'I-can-handle-anything' foundation

I went about creating a list of things I loved to do, I cooked my favourite meals, I made a point of buying my favourite DVDs for when I had a weekend or an evening looming in front of me, I created a calendar of joy and indulgence. I started reading chick lit – something I had always been against as I didn't think it was 'me'. I discovered there was a whole world of delight equivalent to a delicious hot chocolate and cream by sitting and devouring a book that kept the romance alive in me, and let me hope for happy endings.

I want that for you too, I want you to feel that weekends or evenings are a treat not an endurance exercise.

Find out what your love languages are, create a list of all the ways you could fill up your love tank. To give you some ideas, my treat list looked something like this:

* Eating raw cake mix
* Having a candlelit bubble bath
* Having a sweet sherry
* Making my favourite meal of pasta and crème fraiche and courgettes
* Reading a chick-lit book with a hot chocolate and cream
* Saying no to commitments if I felt unsure about them
* Going on the swings in the park
* Going for a Sunday run and having hot baked rolls when I got back
* Pancakes with cream and maple syrup.

I want you to create a list of all the things you love to do in the space below.

_____
_____

## Let's start with loving you

_____
_____
_____
_____
_____
_____
_____

Then create a list of all the things you would want to do but don't because you are waiting for someone to do them with.

_____
_____
_____
_____
_____
_____

What ways could you do the things on your list that would allow you to experience them with or without a partner?

_____
_____
_____
_____
_____
_____
_____

I remember one Sunday, way back. I was on the phone to my friend. We were nattering about the latest films and I said how I wanted to see a film but had no one to go with. My friend suggested I went on my own. I was flabbergasted at

## Creating your 'I-can-handle-anything' foundation

the suggestion and had never even considered it. I thought it would be too humiliating and lonely and embarrassing but I promised her I would try to go to the cinema on my own. I found a local cinema and went to a movie I wanted to see. I was dreading it and I arrived late enough so I wouldn't be sitting on my own waiting for the film to start. I bought a massive popcorn and glass of wine and so began the joy of cinema going on my own. I had no one to share my popcorn with which meant I could eat the lot of it, I could eat it as noisily as I wanted without the worry of irritating a cinema buddy. I saw the films I wanted and on my terms. A quote goes through my head from a Susan Jeffer's book: tasting the delicious sense of independence from doing my own thing. I felt a new me was being born – one who loved going to the cinema on her own!

What activity is a big no-no for you? Is it going to the cinema, a walk on your own in the park, the latest exhibition in the museum? A city break away? What's stopping you enjoying your life right now as it is?

_____
_____
_____
_____

What one step can you make in the next week to step into the life you want?

_____
_____
_____
_____

Let's start with loving you
............................

## Chapter Summary

In this chapter we have looked at decluttering the things holding you back – be it resentments, clutter in your home or old beliefs. We have then looked at self-acceptance and how you can start accepting you as you are right now.

## Chapter 4

# Empowering you to make the most of your life right now

Having perspective when single and dating can be hard. This chapter is all about looking at the choice and the life you have and choosing a way to approach life that works for you.

If we were to float up into a hot air balloon over the road of your life, what would you see? Where are you on your journey?

_____
_____
_____
_____
_____
_____
_____
_____

See how far you've come to this point in your life – think back to the highs the lows, the significant events and day-to-day life that has shaped you to be who you are today. Over your life there have been different phases: living in a particular place, being at university or college, working, travelling. Each stage of life or situation is exactly that – a phase or stage that will at some point end. But when we are in that phase or place it can feel like it will go on forever and that this is your life. We forget to make the most of it until it is too late and we are on to the next phase. It is easy to put blinkers on and be focused on where you want to get to without appreciating the beauty and benefit of the moment.

When you look back at the stages in your life, what do you wish you had done more of or made the most of in each phase?

_____
_____
_____
_____
_____
_____
_____
_____

Now look out into the future. When you're way up in your hot air balloon looking down, a month, a year, a couple of years from now and then looking way into the future to the end of your life, this phase right now feels a smaller part of what's still to come.

When you are up there, looking down, take a breath in and ask yourself, 'what do you know to be true about dating and finding love?' Write down any thoughts and reflections you have in the space below.

## Creating your 'I-can-handle-anything' foundation

_____
_____
_____
_____
_____
_____
_____
_____

We are in the now, and in the now we have a choice. We can choose to wallow, be miserable and to focus on how life will be better once we meet 'the one'. We can choose to ignore the lessons of love we come up against, thus going round and round like a merry go round. Or we can choose another way. I believe if you are reading this book you are looking for another way and I want to help you get there.

I see difficult times as choice points and I too was at a choice point many a time. I was repeating the same patterns, attracting the same dramas and literally had to go through several runs of exactly the same dating experience to actually figure out there was something I wasn't getting. The universe even broke my washing machine so that it was stuck on the first cycle and it would go round and round and round – never finishing the wash – I found that a fitting analogy of the dating cycle I was stuck in.

With this stage of life you have a choice and like every stage in our lives, we all have a choice. Most of the time it either feels like we have no choice or the other extreme, of way too many choices, but we really *do* have a choice. We can choose how we spend our time being single, we can choose who we date, we can choose our mindset. We can choose to focus on the good or on the not so good things going on.

It is all a choice. When we focus on good things happening in our life and focus on gratitude for those things, life has a funny way of getting better.

When I was in my downward misery of not finding love, I would catch myself before sinking too deep, and start back up my gratitude diary. This used to lift me up and change my thinking from being negative and ungrateful, to feeling amazed at the gifts I was getting in my life when my blinkers were off. Things such as getting a seat on the tube to work, seeing a gorgeous sunrise or sunset, having a friend call for a chat or having a delicious breakfast. This is backed up by research which proves that when we focus on the good and are thankful for our blessings in life, we feel more optimistic and happier and it also creates an upwards spiral. We find that we look for more of the good things rather than the problems and negatives in our lives. Also bringing in the law of attraction – when we have a higher vibration (through feeling good in ourselves) we attract more of that good stuff into our lives. It's win-win, but very much a challenge to do when the chips are down and life feels rubbish. In those times, start with doing small things to make yourself feel better, such as cooking and eating your favourite food.

I realised that I could choose to make the most of my time whilst waiting for my life partner or I could have a mopey time and then regret not making the most of my single time after meeting my life partner. It really was my choice though it was easy to forget and slip into fear and worry at times.

And this is what I want for you – *choice* – and being aware of the choice you have in this moment. Being single and free is an amazing opportunity to do what you want with your life and really follow your heart and your dreams.

## Creating your 'I-can-handle-anything' foundation

When we follow our heart and dreams, it puts the focus back onto our growth and development, with the openness that love will come along at the right time, and that in the meantime, this is a phase in your life journey that opens up unique gifts and opportunities for you right now.

In the space below I want you to pause and reflect on what gifts there are for you in being single and dating? What can you do that you couldn't do so easily if you were in a relationship? A good place to start is thinking about your dreams.

If you struggle with knowing your dreams, the next section is for you.

_____
_____
_____
_____
_____
_____
_____

## Dreams

Now is the time to really reflect on what you want to do in life. A good place to start is to create a list of dreams you want to live out and achieve.

_____
_____
_____
_____
_____

*Empowering you to make the most of your life right now*

.............................

_____

_____

_____

When we give ourselves permission to dream, to *really* dream, we get filled with a delicious sense of excitement at the possibilities opening up for us that are available to us if we let them.

Love may come along next week or next year or next decade. You are in the here and now, right now, and this phase in life gives you the chance to shine in some way and grow in some way that wouldn't be possible if you had your life partner there with you. So now is the time to create a life you love, one that is open to a partner coming along but also is a life filled with everything else *you* want to go for.

It can be hard to think about and know our dreams. To help, think back over what dreams you used to have as a child or a teenager? Where did you want to travel to? What did you want to do in life? What hidden passions do you have that are hungering to be expressed?

_____

_____

_____

_____

_____

_____

_____

If you hit against a brick wall, think back to your values activities we did in chapter one. What were your values that you hold true? What would a life rich in honouring these entail?

## Creating your 'I-can-handle-anything' foundation

_____
_____
_____
_____
_____
_____
_____

If it is a struggle to think about the big picture of the life you want to create, break it down into the elements. What sort of home would you be living in? In the country or in the city? What sort of things would you want in your day? Would you want to do something where you are out in nature? Have a corner office in a big company? Working from home? Would you want pets in your life? What kind of activities would you want to fill your day with?

_____
_____
_____
_____
_____
_____
_____

With the questions above (and your values), you are hopefully well on the way to having a list of dreams you would like to fulfil. If you aren't, or are struggling with this, now is the time to look at what's blocking you. What is stopping you and what's coming up around creating a life you want?

Don't be harsh on yourself, take quiet time out. This can help you get the headspace to consider what you want to do. Also it can help to follow what you are curious about.

There are a couple of visualisations in connecting to your future self and life purpose in the bonus information.

A dream list can be a great way to keep track and record what you want to do with your life. I first started my own dream list in New Zealand when I was travelling with an ex and met a delightful couple who had their dreams and hopes with pictures pinned on their fridge to remind them every day of what was important to them. I loved this idea and when a few years later I was single, I somehow was reminded about this dream fridge and decided to create my own. What I discovered was that I had loads of dreams and hopes and wishes that I wanted to fulfil and yes, meeting and marrying my life partner was on my dream list, but so was travelling to India, learning to dance, rock climbing, training to be a life coach, moving to Bath, learning to bake macaroons to name but a few dreams. Suddenly I was fuelled into moving these dreams forward and creating a life I loved. I eventually moved to Bath, found a job I loved, trained as a coach, travelled to India, learnt rock climbing, baked lots of treats (and ate lots of cake mix).

With your list, which ones could you start putting into place right now? Perhaps it's looking into and committing to an evening course in jewellery making, or joining a running club or planning a trip to a far-flung place. Whatever is at the top of your list, start looking at what actions are needed for each one to make it a reality. This may feel daunting, there may be some that are way off where you are now, but having these dreams committed to paper starts sowing the seeds of creating the life you want.

Look around at your life as it is and consider: what you

are putting on hold or putting up with in the bid to wait for the one? Perhaps you aren't putting anything on hold, great if you aren't, but I suspect if you are like a lot of us there are things that are on the back burner. Perhaps it's looking for a new job as your current one, though easy and in your comfort zone, is boring and not stretching you. Perhaps it's your flat; maybe you always dreamed of having your own space but have been putting it off because of costs and just in case you meet someone. Perhaps it's travel and donning your backpack and finally making that trip round the world. Whatever you have been putting off or putting on hold, I ask that you commit to making steps to making those dreams a reality.

Putting things on hold whilst waiting for the right relationship to come along, adds to the sense of deprivation and loss felt in life by not having a partner. I remember when I read Susan Jeffer's *Feel The Fear And Do it Anyway*, she spoke of imagining life as nine boxes to fill. These boxes are areas of our life: career, hobbies, love, home etc. and that by having nine boxes it means that if one box is empty, life still feels really full and there isn't such a gaping hole that there would be if there were only two boxes. What this taught me is that our love life is one box and the lacking in one box doesn't mean that every other of our life boxes should suffer just because our partner is taking their time to show up. How does this fit in with putting things on hold? When we wait for 'the one' before we do things in our life, it adds more weight to finding that special person. It makes it an even bigger stake and bigger loss by their absence or their lack of speed in showing up. So ask yourself honestly, what things are you putting on hold in your life before finding the one? What if you took your 'on hold' list and started making delicious exciting plans for your future? What would they look like? What would that feel like? Thinking about and planning these things can be an exciting step forward.

_____
_____
_____
_____
_____
_____
_____
_____

In what ways can you create the life you want and still keep a space in it ready for your life partner?

_____
_____
_____
_____
_____
_____
_____
_____

You now have your list of dreams or dream board, you are aware of things you are putting on hold in the bid to wait for the one, what about your beliefs?

## Beliefs

Have you ever considered what your beliefs are around finding love, finding the one and creating a life you love?

### Creating your 'I-can-handle-anything' foundation

I would hazard a guess that like most people it isn't top of the agenda of things to do. But the things we believe have a massive impact on the life we create – let me explain.

We all have stories we tell ourselves about how things are. These scripts are handed down to us from our family, friends and society, all telling us how things should be, such as 'it's impossible to find love over thirty', 'it's hard to change into new careers', 'it's hard to save money', 'this is how life is – accept it', 'all men are bad' to name but a few. All too often we buy into how things are and believe our set of beliefs without ever questioning whether they are true, and more importantly, if they are helpful for us becoming who we want to grow into. What happens though is that when we have a belief, a part in our brain called the reticular activating system, filters out any information that doesn't support that belief. So we only get some of the information – the information that supports that belief. So if I believed that the majority of cars were red, I would regularly see red cars, as it is too much for my mind to process all the different types of everything there is in the world.

So how does that link into your life beliefs and dating? If we believe that all men are bad, we attract and only find examples of this. We create that world through the filter of that belief. Sounds a bit out there but stick with me on this. As an example, I believe love is not hard. I believe it isn't meant to be a struggle to be in a loving relationship and I believe things flow when you are with the right person. These are my beliefs and as such I see them manifested in my life. I look at examples around me and only focus on those beliefs that support my own. I actively search out and pay attention to beliefs that support my own. There is a whole host of stuff in our world that goes on without us having any awareness because it is way too much information to absorb all these different beliefs – we'd go insane. When you look at it like that, our beliefs have a massive impact on our world and our experiences.

Take a second. In the space below, what are your beliefs about being single and finding love? Do you see it as easy? Do you see it as impossible? Perhaps you believe all men are untrustworthy or commitment-phobes? If you do, I can guarantee that you are most likely to have experienced these beliefs as fact. Our lives are a mirror, and looking through the eyes of the law of attraction, if we believe something in our heart and soul, the universe has a way of giving us what we believe.

Write a list of your beliefs around love.

_____
_____
_____
_____
_____
_____
_____
_____

What on earth happens if you have uncovered some beliefs that aren't helpful to you finding love? First of all, I want to say, we all have beliefs that aren't helpful for us in some way, shape or form. The key is recognising that the belief isn't helpful and challenging that belief. Take some time to go through the list you pulled together on your beliefs and for each one, ask yourself if that particular belief is helpful in finding true love. If it is then great. If it isn't then now is the time to find examples that disprove that belief. What would be a more helpful belief in helping you find love? Next look at examples that you may have discounted in your own life of when this new belief was held true. Perhaps it's a distant friend who managed to find love at forty-five and is blissfully happy with a baby on the way, or a relative who attracted a lovely gentle committed partner. If you can't find any example in your own life, look further afield – I recommend a quick Google search to find new examples to endorse your beliefs.

Next start becoming aware of when that belief comes up and question yourself when it happens. It is useful to use affirmations here – some examples to get you started are in the box below.

---

*Affirmations when your beliefs are holding you back:*

* I am worthy of love
* I deserve the best right now in my life
* I am confident and capable of being loved
* I am ready now to be loved
* I love me just as I am
* I am proud of what I have achieved
* Available trustworthy men are everywhere.

---

Also creating a little rhyme works a treat with some clients I coach. For example, 'I am lovable and very huggable!' So give it a go and start changing your belief system, or at the very least, question if the belief is what you want to believe in.

We have looked at where you are on your path in life and what dreams you have yet to fulfil. We have looked at how you can start creating a life you love with or without a man in it (but leaving space and room for a partner to come along at the right time). We have looked at your beliefs and how you can change your belief system to help you attract and keep a love you want. Our next section is on goal setting.

## Goal setting and getting to where you want to go

When we know where we want to get to, it can often be challenging to know how to get there. It can feel a long way away from where we are now. So this section is all around goal setting and breaking down your goals into manageable chunks. But before we get into the practical steps, there is a big step in discovering our internal mindset. As mentioned earlier on, research shows there are two types of mindsets: growth and fixed. A fixed mindset means a person is more likely to see their capacity to grow and develop as fixed, so thinking that we only having a certain amount of intelligence or capability. This mindset often comes up with perfectionists, many of us have this perfectionist part. It creates a narrowed belief that things in life are a particular way. A growth mindset looks at challenges and doesn't see them as insurmountable: if a person with a growth mindset fails at something, they see it as a setback, but that they can put effort in to change that and can see that things will change.

The good news is that we can all change our mindset. We can look at the dreams we want to reach and see them as possibilities rather than way off no-hope dreams. By knowing we can change our mindset and being aware of the mindset we tend to adopt, we can make changes and know that we can.

With what you have as an end goal, what tasks need to be done to achieve that goal? Perhaps you have a goal to move to France for a year. Some of the tasks for this could be:

* Learn to speak French
* Investigate areas you want to live
* Research the job market in the areas you like
* Visit the areas you like and narrow down your search
* Make some contacts in the area
* Find the area you want to live.

For each of the steps you've identified, what tasks fall under it? If you need to learn to speak French, perhaps the first step is researching French class options. This could involve the step of speaking to others to gather knowledge and their experience, it could be looking online.

After you have a list of tasks for each step, give a time allocation to each one as to how long you think it would take.

Next print off your calendar and write in deadlines as to when you will be able to achieve the tasks by.

Put deadlines in your diary (on paper and in your phone).

Even though there is a way to get to goals through logical steps, life and ourselves can often get in the way of reaching our goals. This is the time fear will come up and your saboteurs that want to keep you safe and protected will come out in full force with lots of excuses as to why the actions on the to-do list are not important, or it's not the right time. Perhaps your diary will become extra busy and you'll commit to more things than you usually do. Perhaps work will kick off and you'll be too tired to do the things you want in the evening, or you just feel too tired or restless to do the next task on your list. When this happens (as it often does), be prepared for procrastination or for life to get in the way.

> Here are some steps to help you deal with procrastination:
> * First connect into why it is important for you to do this action. What is the final dream you are aiming for?
> * Create a mood board with images to focus in on that final goal
> * Make a playlist that gets you into who you will be when achieving the dream
> * Get a commitment buddy you can have regular accountability catch-ups with
> * Set timers on your phone to do things at certain times or block out chunks of time.

To be honest, if you are wanting to achieve your dream, leg work is needed. It is unlikely to just drop into your lap. Instead you will need to graft to get where you want to get to. But unlike grafting for something you actually don't care about, for example a job you aren't keen on, this is about fulfilling your dream or goal that you'd only dreamed of. It will change you from thinking yourself in one way to see that actually you are able to inspire others. You are able to break through the mundane into a life you love.

## Repeat after me – I'm ready to create a life I love.

Those parts that try to hold us back and stop us (I call them 'saboteurs' and 'inner critics') come up in all of us when we are close to making changes and pushing out our comfort zones. These parts want to keep us safe, knowing this happens helps us see them for what they are.

I want to finish this chapter by acknowledging you for being willing to do the work and look internally at what is going on. It can be tough to look inside and see what we believe in and a whole host of fears can pop up. This is important work to help you find the love that's right for you. It's about believing that love will come along, having faith that it will happen and in the meantime it's creating a life you love.

It's knowing that when you say yes to life, life says yes to you.

## Pause, reflect and next steps check in

We've covered a huge amount in this first section of the book. This part is a chance to take some time to write down any thing you've noticed, anything you want to change, anything new you have learnt about yourself. Feel free to just use the space to write whatever you need to before we move on.

# Relying on you Section

'We do not need magic to transform our world. We carry all the power we need inside ourselves already.' — JK Rowling

## Chapter 5

# Trusting and Using your Intuition

This chapter is about empowering you to tap into your intuition: it's here to give you ways to use this powerful inner resource.

Intuition often gets a bad rap and can be dismissed by society as being nonsense or not real. I believe it is not only real but that it is also an under-used resource in all of us and if we listen and act on our intuition, we can find life is easier.

Accessing your intuition gives you an inner resource, supporting decision-making in your life. But how on earth can it help with dating?

Intuition is something that helps life flow better and by tapping into it when we are dating, it gives us a place within ourselves we can rely on to help guide us. It can help us through the highs and the lows, help us choose what path to take, who to go out with, who to give a chance to, who to trust and who to steer clear of. But intuition isn't just good for dating. By finding that inner wisdom it will give you nudges about what you do in life and how to go about doing it. All too often in my coaching practice, I see clients relying on other people for their opinion and giving away their power to others when making decisions about who to date and what to do in their lives. Learning to trust our inner wisdom means we can be more empowered and confident in the decisions we make. It works to keep us safe and nudge us in the direction that will ensure our growth and be best for us. To be clear, I'm not saying don't listen to your friends and family. Instead, learn to check in with yourself first to know what you feel first before asking others for their opinions, as it muddies the water and makes it hard to hear your own inner voice of wisdom. I feel passionately about empowering you to tap into, trust and act on your intuition, so that it helps you build an inner confidence and leads you in the direction that's right for you.

## What is intuition?

There are many different explanations about what intuition is, ranging from some who believe it is a rational part of our brain, to others who believe it is inner guidance available in all of us – a sense we can all access, but have been taught by society and those around us to not listen to. For me, it is that deep inner knowing inside. The knowing is unlikely to come in delightfully formed, coherently put together sentences. It is more likely to come in feelings, images and symbols that mean something to you. If you're not looking out for the information or aware that it can come in these ways, it can be easily dismissed by the rational mind as nonsense. My experience of intuition is that it comes through as a feeling in my body, or an image, song words in my head, or a smell. Basically, our bodies are the key to accessing our intuition. Our body is our barometer, our channel. Sometimes our intuition is heightened and great in some life situations and not so spot on and developed in other situations. For example, my intuition comes through strongly around danger and keeping safe. This comes through a feeling: I feel my heart getting faster and a pulsing in my lower stomach. When I am coaching I often get visual images and metaphors coming to mind easily. Song words pop into my head which often relate to a situation I am currently going through, when I am on the right path and when I am not. My intuition didn't used to be as strong when dating and in relationships. I would overlook what nudges and warning signs I would be getting from my intuition in a bid to stay in the particular dating situation. I had my blinkers on and I didn't want to believe what I was sensing.

My own journey with intuition has been a varied one. At the age of seven, there was a 'crystallising event' in my life where my intuition was spot on and I courageously acted off the back of it to protect someone I loved. Afterwards I was told off for acting on my intuition. At that age I couldn't understand it and it made me wobble with using my intuition and relying on it. I questioned whether it was right or if I had got it wrong from wrongly listening to the people around me. I believed at that time that I got it wrong. As an adult I look back at that crystallising event and know now that my intuition was spot on, and what I showed was fearless courage and an inner knowing to protect the ones I loved.

As time went on, I thought I had a strong inner guidance, but found I floundered with trusting it. I knew intuitively what was going on: I picked up atmospheres and feelings from others easily, I had dreams that would give me information, I had feelings in my stomach and tingles down my spine that gave me information if I noticed or dared to follow them and

## Relying on you

act on them. I delved into and out of trusting my intuition through my teens and twenties, getting hunches, sometimes following them, but often not. I was good at noticing (on reflection) that my intuition had been spot on, but not on acting on it in the present moment. Does this sound familiar to you? Do you give your power away to others and thoroughly confuse yourself with lots of opinions? I felt unable to trust myself and trust my belief in what I felt, yet always on reflection I knew and sensed what was going on. I put this down to the crystallising event as a child. As an adult, I now know I needed to experience that situation to have that memory of how strong and right my intuition can be and how I need to act on it, despite what goes on around me. I found I shunned my intuition and instead, I gave away my power and decision making to others. This would manifest in me asking lots of people's opinions about what to do, both in dating and in other areas of my life. I found I called up and spoke to lots of my friends, family and actually anyone who I was around who'd listen and give advice. I gathered lots of opinions all of which would make me thoroughly confused and thoroughly unsure of my next step.

In my late twenties I started reading about developing intuition. I sensed that this was important for me in becoming self-aware and growing into a coach. I started becoming aware of when I got a hunch about something. I would write it down and sometimes I would act on it and sometimes I wouldn't. What I noticed was that if I didn't act on my intuition, I would often find that what I had the hunch about would come true. Looking back on my twenties at work I noticed that I was able to juggle a lot of projects, and I would rely on my intuition to nudge me on things I needed to focus on and sort out and what things I could leave on the back burner. I found that when I didn't

## Trusting and Using your Intuition

listen to the inner voice I messed up on my marketing campaigns. I found by keeping track of my intuitive hunches and vocalising to others that I was trusting a hunch, I started trusting my inner guidance even more and became more confident in acting on it.

Initially I was embarrassed about vocalising that I sensed something and was following my intuition or gut for fear of ridicule from others, but the more I read about it and the more I listened to what was going on internally, the more I felt it was important to give credit to my inner wisdom. Why was I conforming and ignoring this incredibly powerful resource within me? I was scared people would think I was weird, too alternative, a bit out there. But luckily there was a stronger fear that if I didn't speak out and vocalise it, then it would never be fully developed and relied on in my life. I started mentioning my intuition and trusting it in front of people. Initially around people who I knew would be a bit more open and who would not belittle it, but over time I talked about it when it came up regardless of the person's response.

I decided to really push my boundaries of trusting my gut to the limits by booking a trip to India on my own. I had been to India before with a friend and knew the craziness and assault on my senses that would greet me. I also knew that for me to really believe in my intuition, I needed to put myself in a situation without friends and family to rely on in a country where I didn't speak the language, and to trust and rely on my intuition to keep me safe. I am not saying that this is what everyone needs to do, just what I needed to do for me to trust myself and build my inner core of belief.

So off to India I went. I met new people, had to sense if I wanted to trust new people, go to places, not go to places. It was an experience I am *so* grateful for. I allowed myself to be in the flow and I did need to rely on it. In one instance on the way home, the hotel arranged for a driver to drive me the five hours to the airport. I was not worried about this as I had booked plenty of taxi drivers before and all had been lovely and respectful. I had got the dreaded Delhi belly and had decided to leave a couple of days earlier to get back to a home I could be happily ill in. The driver picked me up at 4am and I was looking forward to sleeping in the car, but something didn't feel right. I felt uncomfortable with this driver who kept talking about western women being easy. Every conversation, despite where we started, ended up in something sexual. I had a dread in my stomach and knew that this was not a drive to fall asleep in. I got a sense I needed to have my wits about me. I had an urge to make up a 'husband' meeting me at the airport and expecting me. I stayed awake despite being exhausted and him suggesting I rest and sleep. I could feel him watching me in the rear-view mirror. I put a ring on my wedding finger and I stopped engaging in friendly chat. I knew inside that I needed to stay awake for the whole five hours (which was quite a feat for someone who easily falls asleep in cars and had been ill for the last few days with minimal sleep). I got through the journey, I arrived at the airport safely and I thanked the universe for keeping me safe and my intuition for guiding me and urging me to do and say what I needed to: to keep me safe. I found from that experience and my trip to India as a whole, I relied on my intuition more and more in my life. I got into the habit of checking in with myself and acting on what I felt. I also continued vocalising this to others around me to normalise it. I still do this and have found that now it is second nature to check in with my intuition and trust the information I am being given – which can be a challenge when it goes against rational thinking.

## Trusting and Using your Intuition

I want you to pause right now and think of times in your life generally when you have had an inner hunch about something. What was it about? How did it come through to you? Did you follow it? What happened if you did or didn't follow your hunch?

_____
_____
_____
_____
_____
_____

What are your beliefs about intuition? Do you believe in it? Write down what you notice and what comes up for you.

_____
_____
_____
_____
_____
_____

What about dating? Do you get hunches about people and whether you feel like they are the right person for you? Looking back over your relationship history, have you had intuitive hunches that you've ignored or do you act on what feels right instinctively for you?

_____
_____
_____
_____

One of the challenges in listening to our intuition is trying to distinguish the other internal voices going on within us. Sometimes it can feel like a bit of a party inside us – lots of voices, lots of opinions, lots of ways to approach things and it can feel thoroughly confusing to work out which voice is your intuition and which voice is your inner controller or saboteur or cheerleader part of you. One of the ways to start being able to distinguish the inner voices is to notice when the voices come up and the tone of the voice. Our intuitive voice is always loving, knowing and wise. It tends to be a quieter voice, almost a nudge. It may not even come forward as a voice, more a feeling and sense or symbol or picture popping up in your mind. Our intuition is another one of our senses, be it a not so developed sense. Other voices within us can feel very different – they can feel more uptight, more controlling, louder and sometimes more fear based.

To help you to start being aware of what is going on internally, start taking some quiet time out daily. It doesn't need to be lots of time, just ten minutes, to notice what you feel. Why not try a body scan meditation (one available in the free resources online) to bring awareness to each part of your body. If you try this, what you are feeling? Is there any tension? If that part could speak, what would it say?

Bringing your focus to your breath is another way of turning the spotlight on the inner journey. Start being aware and noticing how you feel. If being aware of emotions feels foreign to you, start with simply noticing if you feel mad, bad, glad or sad and naming what is going on. Then when you are used to this, start noticing what the physical sensations are that go with the feeling.

Ask yourself where you feel that feeling strongest in your body. If it had a colour attached to it, what colour would it be? What texture would it have? If it could say something, what would it say?

This all helps to create awareness of what is going on internally so that when we get a physical sensation or image pop into our heads, we are more able to notice it and reflect on what this could mean. It may mean nothing, but it may be your intuition trying to give you a heads up about something.

With dating, get into the habit of checking in with yourself. What was your initial gut reaction when meeting your date? Did you feel a flutter of excitement or a sense of disappointment? Just listen and be aware of what is going on inside you and remember your body is your link to your intuition.

## Ways To Tap Into Your Intuition

Firstly, we *all* have intuition and we can all access our intuition. I see it like a muscle that needs stretching and building up and with practice and acknowledgement it gets stronger. Our bodies are the barometer to get into our intuition, so it is key that our bodies are nourished and looked after like any tool, feeding it nourishing food and plenty of water. Rest and exercise also enable our bodies to be a well-oiled tool and not worn out and frazzled. Find foods that nourish you and become aware of how certain foods impact your body.

Start with bringing awareness to what is going on internally. One of the ways to do this is to start practising bringing attention to your internal world and experience – this can be done through practice. One of the best ways is to bring focus to your breath. When we give ourselves quiet time to just be still, it enables us to look inside and see what's going on. One easy way to do this is to set a timer every day for five minutes and during this time to focus on your breath. Build this up to ten then fifteen minutes. Another way is to practise scanning each part of your body, bringing awareness to what is going on in the body.

What do you feel? Where is your attention drawn in your body? If that part of your body you are drawn to had a message, what would it be? What is it trying to get your attention about?

Get used to checking in with your body when making decisions. A technique that can help with this is imagining the future with the alternative options laid out in front of you like different paths. Imagine yourself going down each path one by one and become aware of how each alternative decision feels in your body. Does a decision make you feel tense or antsy? Visualise making the different decisions and become aware of what comes up internally as you imagine each possibility – this helps tune us in to our inner guidance.

* **Get in tune with your body.** Our bodies give us a host of information and guidance but we often ignore it and are not tuned in to listening to what's going on. To get tuned in with your body, start noticing feelings, tingles and sensations. By bringing awareness to them, it starts us noticing that there is information being given to us. Our bodies are our link to intuition.

* **Do something physical** to get back into your body. Try running, walking, yoga or something where you are using your body and connecting into it, rather than being in your head.

* **Write down intuitive messages you get and keep track of them.** Keeping a small notebook handy with you to write down when you get intuitive hunches about things is a great way to notice and look back on when hunches have come up. Even if we haven't acted on them in the moment, it builds your confidence in its existence.

* **Reflect on your past experiences.** When have you had an intuitive hunch? And has it come true?

* **Start with small things.** Start getting into the habit of checking in with yourself about small things like which movie to see next.

* **Start following urges with dates.** I don't mean jumping-into-bed urges, but more the nudges to spend time with certain people and perhaps reaching out to the person at work that you like but who is shy and tends not to talk much.

* **Put things on the back burner until more information becomes clear.** We can all have a tendency to want to know all the answers in life now, but that isn't how life is. Our intuition often guides us places but doesn't give us the road map as to how this will help us overall. We need to trust that life will turn out well and that our inner guidance is there to bring us the most amazing experiences needed for our growth.

* **Find an intuition buddy** to bounce ideas off of and share with as you develop yours.

The whole point is to start trusting your intuition more and more, especially when it comes to dating. You know what is right for you and really, only you do – it's *your* life. Friends and family around you often have an opinion and it's great to listen to their opinions, but it is also great to get into the habit of checking in with that part inside you that has the wise guidance, as that is the part that knows what is truly right for you.

## Chapter 6

# You're fab, believe it! Your confidence-boosters

Dating and putting ourselves out there can really impact our confidence and self-esteem. It can feel like we have to perform on a date and we only need one bad experience for us to feel like halting on that path and never dating again.

This chapter is all about confidence tools, giving you ways to manage pre-date jitters and ways to build confidence as you step into a life you love.

If we are going to talk about confidence, then fear needs to be addressed as they are closely linked.

Fear is often behind our lack of confidence: fear we will be rejected, fear we aren't attractive enough, funny enough, good enough, fear we will be found out, fear we will be hurt, fear we will hurt someone, fear we will not succeed, fear we will fail in some way. Fear keeps us small and stops us living the life we are meant to live. Fear permeates our lives and we blame confidence on the issue.

The long and short of it is that there is no quick answer to confidence building, but there are ways you can help yourself when you find you are experiencing a confidence-sapping attack.

Let's take a tour round the ways to boost your confidence. There are some quick tools if you find yourself in confidence-sapping situations, and there are some tools to help you connect into confidence in the longer term.

Fear often runs the show in a lot of our lives. We keep ourselves small because we don't want to take risks so life gets even smaller and we take even less risks. Fear makes everything feel scary and our comfort zone becomes smaller and smaller so that we end up living a life that is a shadow of what it could be.

Here's the thing: fear will always come up whenever we are trying to put ourselves into situations that are new to us. As Susan Jeffers says, we need to 'feel the fear and do it anyway'. Fear will always be a part of our lives when we want to do something new. It comes up in procrastination, in saying we don't want to do something when secretly deep down we do. Fear can run circles round us and keep us small. But lovely, that is not your path and I suspect if you are reading this chapter you want to find an alternative way to handle fear so that you can put yourself out there and feel more confident.

## Fear

Fear shows up when we are doing something new or pushing into a new territory or doing something that makes us feel vulnerable and exposed. Dating often hits every one of the panic buttons inside us as we are needing to constantly put ourselves out there and meet new people with the fear of rejection, ridicule and misery going on inside us.

But if fear is always there when we are doing something new, what on earth can we do?

Hard as it sounds, we need to make friends with fear and learn how to be with it, regardless of what is going on around us.

'Being with fear' sounds a bit crazy. We all wish there was a magic wand we can wave that will make fear disappear, but there isn't. The only way to get over fear is to go ahead and do the thing you are scared about, and then you don't feel the fear so much as you've managed the things you are scared about. But fear will then come up in another situation as you push and expand your comfort zone into creating a life you love.

## Working with fear

**Make friends with fear.** Imagine meeting your fear – what would it look like? Be aware of the resistance you feel and know you can always go back to being resistant to it, but for the moment try putting aside resistance and greeting your fear with love. What happens when you do this? What happens to the fear? Often it becomes smaller.

Start being aware of where fear lives in your body, what shape it is, what colour it is, what texture it is, if it had a message for you what would it be? What image comes to mind when you are thinking about fear? It helps to personify fear.

Get to know and understand your values – what is important to you? Through using your values as a guide and a compass, they guide the way. So when we're feeling in the midst of the gloom of fear they shine a beacon of light guiding us home. Go back to chapter 2 to look at values.

Notice the fear – if it had an image attached to it, what would that image be? What message would it have for you? When we look at our fear face on and explore it, we allow ourselves to get comfortable with fear and it has a funny way of not being quite so scary.

Write down the things that you are afraid of – all of the things, yes every single one of your life's challenges that bring up fear. With each one, breathe deeply and ask yourself 'what does this part of me need right now to move forward?' Pause and allow yourself to listen, *uncensored*, to the answer. Fear often stems from our vulnerability and the need for reassurance and love. When you have an answer, reflect on what you could do to give yourself what you need so that you feel more comfortable in the fear-inducing challenge.

What is one thing you can do today that would be a step to overcoming a fear? I challenge you to do it and see what happens. Yes it will feel uncomfortable, but once you've done that one thing, the fear will be that little bit smaller and will have a little less hold over you and who you want to be.

When we are aware of our fears, we know what is holding us back and we can start using the techniques above to manage fear. This enables us to start feeling more confident and less afraid of our big bad fears.

In what situations do you feel you lose confidence? Is it before a date? On the first date? On the second date when you feel you're going to disappoint? Is it at work? When you are going for things you only dreamed of?

A lack of confidence can manifest in a number of ways. Perhaps it's procrastination or keeping to what you know because of the potential risks involved. It could be that the physical manifestations of this is sweaty palms, shaking, shrinking into yourself in a bid to not be seen.

## Confidence boosters

What would be your physical position of confidence and self-assurance? Perhaps it is standing tall with feet and arms hip width or perhaps it's sitting up and shoulders back. To find yours, ask yourself, what is the posture of confidence? Then what is *my* posture of confidence? Then get into the posture of how confidence comes through for you.

There has been some interesting research on this from Amy Cuddy on the power pose. When we adopt a confident pose, we send a message to every cell in our body that we are confident, which in turn helps us to become more confident. Check out Amy Cuddy on YouTube to find out more.

By practising your confidence posture everyday (and in particular when you feel unconfident) it gives you an automatic way to connect into confidence. If you struggle with finding your confident posture, have a think about who you know who is confident and how they appear. Is it their physical stance that makes them confident? Or is it what they say? Or how they say it?

How can you use this on a date? Find where confidence lies in your body. Some clients find this is in their stomach, shoulders or throat. Imagine it had a colour, a texture, a shape. What would it be? By visualising this confidence when you need it, and imagining it growing and expanding through your body, it can help with feeling more confident.

Become aware of your inner voices. What comes up when you are feeling unconfident? Is it that you aren't good enough, aren't pretty enough? Tall enough? Intelligent enough? Become aware of these inner messages and ask yourself with each one: Is it true? Is it absolutely true? What alternative messages can you repeat when those thoughts pop into your head?

* Reflect. Ask yourself, when was a time I did really well? Develop a confidence scrap book, full of images, letters, certificates and other things that remind you of what you can achieve and how well you have done in the past. When you are feeling like you need a boost, get the scrap book out and remind yourself of your achievements.
* Visualise. When you are going to be in a situation that makes you feel unconfident, imagine the best outcome and everything going well. See it as a film being played out in your mind. Our mind doesn't know the difference between us actually doing something or visualising doing something. Research shows we can produce new networks in our brain and strengthen our muscles just by visualising. The key is repetition, to keep running through the visual in your mind when you can.
* Practise focusing on your breath. When you are in a situation that makes you apprehensive and anxious, focus on your breath. I mention this a lot in my blog posts because it works, believe me!

## Quick Jitter Fixes

* **Wear clothes that make you feel confident.** Sounds a basic idea, but wearing clothes that look good, (i.e. aren't too tight, aren't badly fitting, aren't old and shabby) will help build our confidence. When we are wearing things that just don't make us feel great, it comes out in our posture, our way of being and the things we say. It doesn't need to be expensive but find a first date outfit (and second date outfit) that makes you feel fantastic, sexy, full of life.

*You're fab, believe it! Your confidence-boosters*

* **Wear a perfume** that reminds you of confidence and feeling good. Smell is a great way to connect us into who we are and anchors us to particular feelings, I used to have a date perfume that reminded me that I was in date mode.

## Practise saying in the mirror – I am me and I am confident

* **Connect to your breath.** I say it regularly, but connecting to your breath is a great way to anchor you when you are feeling jittery. Practise breathing in for a count of four and out for a count of six. By making the out breath a longer breath, it calms the heart and the body into rest mode.

* **Send loving kindness to yourself and your date.** Before going on the date, practise a loving kindness meditation to send love to yourself and to your date. You can find a script for this in the box below.

---

*Loving kindness Meditation*

*First of all there is no right or wrong way of doing this meditation. There are different ways - some bringing in everyone you know others focusing on one or two people - do what feels right for you. This is how I do the meditation, adapt it as it feels right for you.*

---

Sit comfortably. Begin relaxing your whole body by breathing in for a count of four and out for a count of six. Close your eyes and bring your awareness inward. Without straining or concentrating, just relax and be.

Take a deep breath in. And breathe out.

Bring to mind someone you love very much, imagine that person is in front of you and say either out loud or in your head;

'May you be loved'
'May you be happy'
'May you be at peace'

Allow yourself to really feel the love.
Bring to mind all your friends and loved ones in a group and repeat the wishes.
Next say to yourself 'May I be loved, may I be happy, may I be at peace.'
Next bring to mind someone you feel neutral about and repeat the phrases;

'May you be loved, may you be happy, may you be at peace.'

Then bring to mind someone who challenges you, perhaps someone who has hurt you or upset you, repeat the same wording.
I often finish the meditation imagining all the people I have wished love towards to be there in a group and I imagine the love and wishes flowing from me to them.
Take a deep breath in and out and open your eyes.

* **Reframe the date in your mind.** As I mentioned in chapter four, we can often get stuck in certain perspectives and ways of being. If you were to change the perspective that you viewed dating through when it comes to confidence, what lens could you adopt that would help? Some people find that if they look at the date through the lens of their favourite film hero or playful fun lens, then it helps them to see the date and the nerves in a different way. To get into a different lens, think about your favourite film or a hero you admire. Then try on the lens of what a date would be like through their eyes. What would they say? What would they do? How would they be?

  By looking at the date through a different lens, it opens up the choices we have when we are on the date as to how we put ourselves across.

* **Scripting.** Write out what you want to happen. This helps to make you clear about what you want from your date. It doesn't need to be too long or detailed, just a positive version of what you'd like to happen.

* **Shake it out.** Often we can get lots of energy going on inside of us and when we are nervous it can come out even more, so go somewhere where you can shake the energy out. Shake your arms and legs, do a little jog if it helps.

Confidence seems elusive – something some people have it and others don't, but I want to share with you that we all have the capacity to be confident and become the people we want to be. You need to let go of your doubts (with the help of techniques shared in this book) and be comfortable in your own skin, being the amazing unique you that you are.

# Date-smart

'F. L. Y. First Love Yourself, Others will come next.' — Unknown

## Chapter 7

## Dating words of wisdom

You have worked on identifying the amazing things about you that will help you love and accept yourself as you are right now. We also looked at boosting your resilience, what you want from life and using your inner resources and wisdom to get it. A lot has been covered – fab work for sticking with it as it's challenging looking deeply and honestly at ourselves. If you are out there dating or thinking about dating soon then this chapter is here to arm you with some of the things that I've found help me and others I know. You are at this stage of the book and have an idea about what you are looking for in a partner and what you have to offer.

When I think back to my dating it was, at times, scary stuff. I felt I needed to build myself up before every date and I never knew what would greet me. I attracted all sorts of crazy commitment-phobes, but I suspect that was also the energy I was putting out at the time. The 'I'm not truly ready, but I will half-heartedly date' vibes. Dating used to take over my life, but later on I tried to get more balance back.

I did most of my dating through online dating sites. I also had the occasional blind date and met men randomly at weddings and nights out.

So first things first – be honest – what are you looking for at the moment? Do you want to find your life partner? Are you wanting to date but don't want a serious relationship? Are you *ready* for a long-term relationship?

Sometimes it is hard to nail down the stage we are at and what we want to find regarding love, and some people would be of the opinion we need to be open to whatever comes along. To save yourself some heartache, it helps to really reflect on what it is you actually want, because subconsciously you will be attracting it in some way even if consciously you aren't aware of it.

This chapter is mainly for those wanting to find a loving long-term relationship – it has dating wisdom I have learnt, but with everything, it may or may not be right for you. I want to share my experiences with you but you may find something very different that may be more right for you.

After my year of being single, I was definitely ready to mingle and I thought I was relatively ready to find love. I went on a few dates and started getting myself out of the haven of a home I had created, and like a butterfly spreading her wings for the first time, I was starting the process of what I'll call my 'crazy dating stage'. I went on a couple of dates with someone who was unhappy in work and life; the date felt more like a coaching session. It was confirmation of the joy and flow I felt when empowering others to get onto their right path, but it wasn't what I wanted in a relationship. I ended it with the Mr 'unsure of which path to take' and was proud of myself for breaking another relationship pattern (be it a two-date relationship!):

me actually ending a relationship rather than waiting for someone else to end it. I had a choice, which takes me onto lesson one.

## Datewise One

*Not settling for second best.*

I hope from the work you've been doing in previous chapters on increasing your self-love and acceptance, that 'not settling for second best' is something you are on the path to stopping. I feel it's important to flag this as the first lesson because it's a trap we can all very easily fall into.

I want for you to find that all-encompassing love, to find your soulmate, to find the one that really makes your heart sing. But fear creeps into all of us – 'what if I don't have a special someone?', 'what if I'm not lovable?', 'what if I never find him/her?' Fear keeps us from saying what we really want and fear gets us settling for second best.

If you are dating someone and deep down you just don't know and are unsure about him/her, listen to your inner voice and wisdom. What is it saying? I found I was giving men chances and then falling for them, but actually deep down I knew they weren't right.

Sometimes we know that they aren't right and in the bid to be with someone – anyone – we can have a tendency to just accept and put up with things we just don't want to compromise on (but *are* compromising on).

Listen to what *you* feel and keep track in your journal. After every date I would write down all the things I liked and any clues that could mean the person wasn't right for me. I am not saying you don't give a person a chance, just be aware and alert to any warning signs so you are going into this with your eyes open.

You are potentially going to be spending the rest of your life with this person so it is key they are right for you. It's not about waiting for the most perfect partner in the world, just don't settle. Clichéd as it sounds it does feel different with 'the one'. When I first started dating my hubby I had warning signs: he was a few years younger and I wondered if this meant he wouldn't be at the stage I was in wanting to settle. He seemed like he loved the London life and yet I was in Bath – how would that work? He seemed quiet (was that a sign of him not being interested, or worse still a commitment-phobe?). He didn't put a x on his texts, did that also mean he wasn't interested? I remember talking to my lovely friend Julia about whether he liked me. She suggested an alternative: that he may have just been shy and quiet and to give him a chance. It turned out he was quiet and shy. My point being that I listened to the potential warnings and had them on my radar, but I did not rule him out straight away (thankfully).

This lesson I share with caution as I don't want you to rule out potential fab partners, but if you have a pit of dread in your stomach, an inner-knowing voice you are ignoring, then I beg you to listen and don't do it. I know of a few people who had that feeling of dread on their wedding day. They knew the marriage wasn't what they wanted, but went along with it to prevent disappointing others. But disappointing others is nothing to the disappointment you'll feel if you find yourself meeting your soulmate, but are unhappily married to another person.

I know we all have that fear, compounded by the media that we need to get moving due to the impending doom of the biological clock. But hang on, lots of women have babies and families at different times in their life in some way, shape or form – if that is what they want. I remember having a conversation with one of my friends about the time I would start the egg freezing process to ensure I could be a mother yet not settle for second best in the love department because of it.

It helps with this lesson if you are clear about what you want and what relationships and types of people don't work for you. If you're not sure, spend time reflecting and journaling on your experiences to date and what has and hasn't worked for you.

## Datewise Two

*There needs to be more than just the 'lovely' factor.*

Avoid sticking with men who are lovely just because they are lovely (this one closely links to lesson one). Most of us want to find a lovely man, but just because they are nice doesn't mean they are the one. I regularly fell for nice men because I thought that I wouldn't get hurt and that a lovely man is not to be passed up. I remember my wise brother-in-law saying to me, 'just because they are lovely, doesn't mean they are right for you'. His point being that there are lots of nice people he could name as being 'nice', but they would not be compatible in a relationship. There needs to be more than that. Sounds a straightforward enough lesson, but when you've had the umpteenth bad date and finally you come across a man who is nice, there is a part of you that sings hallelujah and doesn't want to pass up a 'lovely' man despite him not having anything else you want in a life partner.

In addition to this, don't feel guilty letting go of a lovely man and passing him up. It doesn't mean you are ungrateful, picky or difficult. It means you know what you are looking for and what is important to you. I reaffirm that it is important to have that strong foundation of self-acceptance and assertiveness, as everyone will have an opinion on what or who is right for you. I also strongly believe that if we all were honest about love and did not settle, everybody would have a shuffle around and end up with their soulmates. We all need to step over the fear.

## Datewise three

*Be true to you.*

It sounds simple enough but in order to be liked we can often project another persona out to the world, especially when dating. Halfway through the dating years, I noticed I was in a pattern of being really nice and sweet and quiet (previously I had been told I was 'too much' and wanted to be accepted and fit in), then as I went on my dates the real me came out and boy were they in for a surprise. I am sometimes sweet, but I'm also pretty fiery and strong-willed with strong opinions. The men would run for the hills and in a vicious loop of proving the point: being myself proved I was unlovable. By not being my true self from the start, men thought I was a particular way, which I wasn't. Men thought they were getting something different to the real me.

I ask you to pause and think about which version of 'you' you are projecting on dates. Are you being sweeter than you are, suppressing opinions or moods? Are you being particularly outgoing and attracting a particular type of man, when really you love a quiet night in and the joy of silence?

What helped me, was starting to unpick the stories and beliefs I had that were keeping me in that limiting persona. I found that I believed deep down that I was too much to handle being the real me. I was not lovable and acceptable having strong alternative views. I remember being told by one family member that I needed to tone down my alternative side to be able to find love. I even had one date say that he could not be with someone who believed in the universe and such like. Luckily at that point when I heard that advice and dated that man, I knew it was not helpful advice. So if you have received such advice from those around you, I want you to write down all that is wonderful and amazing about you. Look at the list and ask yourself, who is the real you that is itching to get out and be expressed in life and in dating? How can you let that real you come through in your life?

I knew for me to be authentic I needed to be able to talk freely and openly about trusting my intuition, about believing in such things like the universe, or destiny. I needed to be able to express myself by having crystals around my home and to have and share my hopes and dreams and passions in becoming a life coach – my real hopes and dreams not the ones I thought others would be impressed by hearing. All this made me vulnerable, vulnerable in being rejected and vulnerable in not being liked for who I am. But by being me and allowing the world to see me as I am, helped me become more confident in myself to show up in the world as me and not afraid of what people thought.

## Datewise four

*Look out for wrong men packaged up as new men.*

This one caught me out a few times. I knew I was attracted and drawn to controlling, cocky, sometimes arrogant know-it-alls that believed they were superior and better than those around them. But when I started dating again, I noticed that time and time again that same type would come back up, but look slightly different so I would think they were a new type of man. This is where listening to your inner guide and keeping a journal with any thoughts and potential watch outs is helpful. I broke the pattern through awareness (and blimey did I have to go on dates with quite a few wrong men for me to realise this pattern existed). I also worked on my self-love and acceptance. I knew I must have been feeling pretty unsure of myself to be attracting such men, especially as I seemed to attract men that loved to criticise me. I knew this meant I had work to do on my self-love.

If you recognise a pattern, go back over the exercises in the self-love section. Awareness is the first step in breaking any pattern and when we are aware, we are then in a place of choice.

## Datewise five

*Go with what YOU feel, not what others advise.*

I can't state this lesson loudly enough. When you're single and also putting yourself out in the world, it can feel like a maze of choices and fear can creep up around making the wrong decision. We can feel more ungrounded than usual and more out of touch with our intuition and wisdom, so we ask for others' opinions.

This was a favourite mistake of mine. I would ask opinions, but also family and friends would give me their unsolicited opinions on situations. All this added up to me feeling thoroughly confused and unable to clearly hear my own inner voice and unable to really connect in with what was right for me.

If you find yourself relying on your friends or family to make decisions around your love life, start taking back your power. This can be as simple as getting into the habit of checking in with yourself before asking for opinions of others so that you can tap into and listen to what you are thinking and feeling. If your life is anything like mine there will be plenty of opinions around you on what is good for your life. I'm not saying that some of this advice isn't helpful, just that to fully own your choices and decisions and step up to being the empowered person you can become – it is about knowing what you want. Also, be aware of wanting to please. I know I had a strong desire to make my mum proud of me, so I looked for approval for the decisions I was making when really, on reflection, I can see that I didn't need the approval and that I know what is best for me. And when I don't know what is best for me, I will learn from my mistakes and will soon know what is best for me.

I will add into this lesson that it also helps to be aware of flattery from dates. Everyone loves a bit of flattery, but I noticed whilst dating that actually I easily succumbed to flattery and ended up going on a few dates more than I would have with some of the men, even though I was not sure of them. I almost side-stepped my feelings and my wants and desires in exchange for being told I was pretty and a great package etc. I can see now how that gave an indication as to where I was with my self-love. I wonder what a different pattern I would have adopted had I been more loving and accepting of me.

## Datewise six

*Be aware of jumping into a relationship because you want a relationship – any relationship.*

For me, patience is something I need to constantly work on and at the beginning of a relationship when a person would come along, I wouldn't always wait to find out if they were right. I would jump feet first into believing they were the one. I would fall for the idea of a relationship and not actually check if *they* were right. I soon realised that this was causing me more heartache than necessary so started dating smart, which is what our next chapter is all about.

To end this chapter here is a brief re-cap of the lessons learnt:

- ♥ Don't settle for second best (if you struggle with this, take a look back at the self-love chapter)
- ♥ There needs to be more than just the lovely factor
- ♥ Be true to you
- ♥ Look out for wrong men packaged up as new men
- ♥ Go with what you feel not what others advise (the chapter on Intuition can help on this)
- ♥ Be aware of jumping into a relationship just because you want a relationship (if you struggle with this, take a look again at how you can keep your love tank full so that there is less urgency to jump into any relationship)

## Chapter 8

## Dating – Preparing for your date/tapping in to your inner dating goddess

In this chapter we will look at the preparation you can do to help you before you go on your date.

I found that getting ready for a date used to give me loads of butterflies (and sometimes a big ball of dread in my stomach) for what would await me. Here are some ways I prepared myself that I found helpful that could also help you:

♥ Have a list of date topics you feel comfortable chatting about. For me my job, hobbies, travel and food were things I loved to speak about. It helped for me to have a couple of topics I could ask them about as well. I used to love finding out how they spent their Sundays. I felt it told me a lot about the type of person they were. Were they a snuggle-in and batten-down-the-hatches for a quiet day type, or were they an out and about meeting friends and family type of guy? It all gave me clues as to what they liked to do with their time. Being enthusiastic about cooking and food, I also found it fascinating to find out about their cooking and culinary tastes. I love good food and I knew from experience that for me, being with someone who also loved good food was important.

- ♥ What is on your list of topics? What do you love doing and are passionate about that you could easily chat and share with another? Here's a short list to get you started.

---

**Date Topic Ideas:**

1. How do you like to spend a day off?
2. What's your perfect Sunday?
3. What are your favourite all time movies? And why?
4. Do you like to cook and if you do what is your favourite meal to make? Why?
5. Tell me about your job.
6. What do you like doing out of work/in spare time?
7. Have you always lived in xx?
8. What is on your bucket list? And why?
9. Where would you like to visit in the world?
10. Where is your favourite place to chill and relax?

---

- ♥ Have a 'build me up' playlist playing when getting ready for your date. For me, this would remind me of all the fabulous things about me. It felt great having a sing and dance in my flat to songs such as 'I Am Woman', 'I Have Confidence' and a bit of cheesy S-club 7 'Reach'. It helped me to dance and sing out my pre-date jitters and it also helped to fill me up with positive feelings. Listening to this playlist whilst walking to meet my date helped me as well. The Girls Aloud song 'The Promise' made me feel attractive and slinky and to feel like the gorgeous lady that I

knew deep down I was but often struggled to get in touch with.
- ♥ Read through your list of all the wonderful qualities you have to offer a partner. This can help to remind you how fab you are and that you are definitely dateable and more than that: a bloody good catch!!
- ♥ Scripting: Write out the best possible way the date could go. What will you feel, what will you do and the connection you'll make. Focus completely on how it makes you feel and find that feeling in your body. Imagine it growing and spreading – starting like a fizz of excitement or joy or anticipation and allow it to grow and permeate every cell in your body. This helps to connect into what the date will be like. When I do this with other areas in my life, I find that things often work out the way I visualise. There is something about expecting the best to happen that, in a magical way, puts the energy and intent out there. It's doing it in a non-attached way but really visualising the best that could happen.
- ♥ Using quotes and sayings also helped in my prep for dates. I loved the Susan Jeffers's quote 'as I say yes to life, life says yes to me!' And also the saying 'if life gives you lemons, make lemonade!' These helped me to focus on making the best of situations and when I am focused on the positives, it helped me to remain grateful. I also remember reading a gorgeous book a few years ago in which the lead character used the strategy of finding three positives in every situation. Even if I haven't used this religiously in every situation, it helped me focus more on the positives.
- ♥ What would your sayings be to keep you feeling filled with confidence and energy for your date? If you are struggling for ideas, see the box below.

## Date-smart

**Quotes and Sayings:**
- ♥ I love all that I am just as I am
- ♥ Stars don't shine without darkness
- ♥ I believe in love
- ♥ 'Don't compare your beginning to somebody else's middle' – Jon Acuff
- ♥ I was given this life because I was strong enough to live it
- ♥ I'm not single, I'm not taken, I'm simply on reserve for the one who deserves my heart
- ♥ Don't lose hope – you don't know what tomorrow will bring
- ♥ You have to love the life you live, not mourn the life you wish you had

## Chapter 9

## Date Smart

Dating smart is about empowering you to make choices that fit with your relationship aspirations. I hope that by sharing these tips, it will help you have more success with dating and learn from some of the errors I made.

## Tip One

*Look out for déjà vu moments on your date.*

You know the moments when you feel like you have been there before and had the same date already. This is probably because you *are* on the same date in some way, shape or form. This is your clue from the universe that something needs to change as you are still attracting and going for the same type. If you recognise this, go back to the chapter on self-love and look at what beliefs come up and work on this.

## Tip Two

*Notice where your energy goes.*

Do you find you are asking lots of questions? Listening a lot? Giving a lot of you? Be aware of energy drainers who take, take, take, but aren't willing to put the effort into the relationship.

In my own dating past, this was up there as one that I was most guilty of. I was eager to please, texting my dates regularly, not playing games, coming up with lots of conversation and if they didn't call, following them up by text. This behaviour was even worse after I had had a couple of dates with a guy. It was almost like I was trying to prove my worthiness as girlfriend material. One day I was wondering why I was so drained and came to the realisation that I was putting in all the effort and actually not getting much back. I started leaning back a little; not a big amount and certainly not in the sense of playing games (which I will come onto shortly) but in the sense of me not working so bloomin' hard to prove I was worthy. Leaning back helped me to feel less drained of energy and more able to get some perspective on whatever dating situation I was in.

If this is something you notice in yourself, I want you to pause and think about how you can start noticing when you are putting too much effort into a relationship. What are your warning signs you could spot in advance?

My signs were that I used to start feeling resentful and drained, I would be more anxious and ungrounded, jumping from one thing to the next. I also knew when I started asking for lots of opinions from those around me. It was often a sure fire way to know I was out of balance and in need of a serious battery recharge. When I have ignored all the warning signs, I have been known, on more than one occasion, to just explode like a grenade. It's almost like the resentment needed an outlet. If you find yourself exploding there are some great ways I have learnt that you can use to manage the energy build up in ways that mean you're not on the back foot. Take a look at this in the box on this page.

> **Ways to help you release pent up energy and emotion:**
>
> ♥ Do something physical – go for a fast walk, run, boxercise class – anything that gets you pounding the energy out
> ♥ Belt a tune out – at the top of your voice
> ♥ Shake out the energy – be somewhere where you won't be disturbed and shake your limbs
> ♥ Try EFT – there are lots of free EFT videos online. Try searching for ones on releasing pent-up energy
> ♥ Grab a pillow and scream into it at the top of your voice (it helps to do this when no one is around so you can release your inhibitions).

## Tip Three

*Try not to snog their face off all evening.*

If you are physically attracted to your date, try not to snog them too early on. It sounds a bizarre one this, but if you like someone, take the time to get to know them so that they see you as more than just an advanced tonsil-hockey champion. When I actually found myself on a date with a man who was physically attractive, sometimes I was so overcome with relief (phew not another frog) and gratitude that I actually felt something for him. I would be happy to snog his face off part way through date one and subsequent dates. This is all very well and good, but I found it didn't really give me a chance to actually sit and get to know them without my desires getting in the way and muddying the waters. If you are looking for a life partner, it is key to check for sexual compatibility (and yes kiss them), but I found that balance is key – balance to find out more than if he has a good kissing technique, balance to let him find out more about you and balance for you both to decide if there is chemistry to go on more dates. This leads me nicely onto my next tip…

## Tip Four

*Try to avoid having sex too early.*

Challenging as this one may be, try to avoid having sex if you see yourself being with this person in the longer term. As with too much snogging, sex definitely muddies the waters when trying to figure out if you're a good fit with someone. Though I definitely think that sex is a massive part in compatibility, it can also get attachment tied up in the mix. I know I fell foul of this rule a few times in my dating past and wondered why I wasn't getting anywhere with men if I slept with them. When it comes to dating I found it didn't help me find love, it just confused the issue and made me feel bad and sometimes used. I found I was getting attached way too soon and attached to men who weren't right for me. If you find yourself in a pattern of sleeping with men after a couple of dates, ask yourself what it is you are looking for from sex. Is it the physical connection? Is it the intimacy with someone? Is it the thrill of being wanted? Ask yourself how could you get that without the need to have sex. Is it regular massages so that you have the physical contact you require? Or cuddles from an understanding friend (not a friend with benefits)? Try holding off until you are dating regularly and feel that they are committing wholly to the awesome woman that you are.

## Tip Five

*Beware of ex chat – either from you or your date.*

Dating is about finding out about someone and them finding out about you, so that you can both figure out if you are a good match. Definitely knowing about their relationship history is important, but watch out for talking too much about your exes. If you find they are talking too much about their exes, it could be a warning sign for still being in love with exes or having unresolved issues that could come up and rear their ugly heads in your potential relationship.

I remember dating someone for a couple of months. Let's call him 'Mr Miserable And Still In Love With My Ex' man. I should have listened to the signs: on date one the aforementioned ex was mentioned. He loved to tell me details of their relationship and that she was 'his own personal brand of heroin'. Obviously music to a potential girlfriend's ears (not) but I gave him the benefit of the doubt and still allowed and accepted this ex talk. When I went to his house and saw old love pictures they had drawn for each other still up on the wall, I started getting the distinct feeling that this 'Mr Miserable And Still In Love With My Ex' was in fact still in love with his ex (surprise surprise).

When there is an ex hangover going on, it creates issues with one or both of you not being fully in the relationship and also not being fully present. It can also make you feel rubbish and like you have to live up to the unrealistic view of the ex, when my lovely one, you deserve a partner who is fully into you and committing to you and only you!

This can also go the other way too. I know at the start of dating I occasionally used to bring up exes and talk about exes. I think there was a part of me that liked to reminisce, but also a part of me that felt good if the person showed any jealousy. It made me feel that they liked me. Now I can see that by holding my energy and attention on an ex, my energy and attention wasn't free to focus on what I wanted from a new relationship. I'd be still in the reminiscing, so it comes as no surprise that I put men off with this chat and also I ended up attracting men who were similar to the ex I had broken up with. I was being caught in that same relationship pattern and wondering why on earth things weren't working out. If like me, at times you have or are struggling to let go of an ex boyfriend, take a look at my chapter on Breakup survival to find tools on removing the ex from your thought patterns and move on.

## Tip Six

*Date smart and look out for clues about your date.*

Does your date say they want to find true love and a long-term relationship, but their behaviour is perhaps suggesting they are still up for playing the field? Do they say they are interested yet rarely call you, leaving you to do all the chasing? Do they say they are looking to commit and settle down yet their longest relationship is literally weeks or days? As a *date smart* person, you need to look for clues beneath the surface, trust your intuition and listen to what they say and how you feel. Does it all add up or does something not sound or feel quite right? When I went out with 'Mr Blind Date' man he was making all the right noises. He said that he was looking for love and wanted to settle down and I fully believed him because I really wanted it to be true. But digging beneath the surface I noticed he was making all grand gestures for the future (suggestions that we book a holiday, spend a weekend away, get bikes to go cycling together, visit this and that place together), but actually things were not adding up to what was being promised. He wasn't calling when he said he would and wasn't committing in the present moment. I missed the clues until we were a month or three down the line and the writing was clearly on the wall – I failed to listen to my intuition. Save yourself the time by making sure you tap into your intuition and senses about whether this person is what they say they are.

## Tip Seven

*Enjoy the date but please don't turn it into an interview!*

This sounds like a no-brainer, but when you've been on countless bad dates, it can feel like the best way to get through them is to ask the questions that you want to know the answers to without the pleasantries in between, then decide if the answer is what you want to hear and move on if not! But hey, wait a minute lovely! If you are interviewing someone with numerous questions, they will feel like it's an interrogation and this won't be bringing out the best in them. I know at points I was on the receiving end of being questioned and it doesn't feel great. It made me nervous, closed off and unwilling to participate in whether I ticked all their boxes. I remember on one particular date, halfway through 'the interview', the man was asking if I could cook then visibly relaxed when he heard the answer was yes. To me he wasn't asking or interested in food and the delights of good cooking. I got a sense this was to tick the box 'she is house trained and able to look after me'. This was a complete turn off. I was being judged for something that for me, really wouldn't be that important when you're with the right person.

Be date smart and look out for those rogue daters who want to tick certain boxes and look for the perfect partner. Delicious food is and always will be incredibly important to me. From the outward signs when I first met my husband, he was not what I was 'looking for' in this area. He ate out a lot and when I first went to his shared bachelor pad, I was quite taken aback about the pizza boxes and general lack of cooking going on. By not taking things at face value and delving beneath the surface, I actually found out that he loved home-cooked food but his current lifestyle wasn't giving him that outlet to cook. Imagine my surprise and delight when I heard from his family that actually he loved cooking and used to relish watching and learning from cookery programmes. What I could have been closing myself off to if I had stuck with the blinkers of my tick list. So reflect back on how you date at the moment. Do you have fun and bring curiosity to the date or does it feel like an interview? Or maybe somewhere in the middle? Become aware of what you want and what you are putting out there.

## Tip Eight

*Bring your curious self to your date.*

I know at times I was guilty of zoning out on a date – thinking of the things I needed to do when I got home and thinking of the reasons they were not right. But dating is an opportunity to meet and learn something new about another human being and to become excited about new experiences. If you zone out, there is probably a reason. Generally when we are interested and enjoying our time we stay alert and in the situation, but if you are on a date and find yourself zoning out – not just once, but several times, alarm bells should be ringing.

## Tip Nine

*Don't get too serious too quickly.*

Commit but have fun! I always used to think that being committed was being serious and talking about serious things on a date. I would be itching to find out how many children they wanted or where they wanted to live when they settled. I found I was having serious conversations about this deep stuff with men I barely knew. I didn't even know what their favourite film was or figured out if we were right for each other, but I certainly knew if they wanted children and how many. All that changed when I met my husband. For the first time ever I had real fun on my dates. Gone were the serious conversations. Instead our dates involved fun filled activities that were crazy and silly and light-hearted. I didn't know if he wanted children and I didn't know where he wanted to live and settle or even if he wanted to settle. What I did know is that I had fun and he called and sent texts when he said he would. He would arrange dates, he committed to see me at the weekends and I felt secure yet was having fun. This was a real difference for me. I wasn't having the full-on commitment chat but I loved his company, and he was committing. He didn't say he was madly in love with me (at the beginning) but he did want to arrange the next date, he did call and text. This leads me onto the next tip...

## Tip Ten

*Avoid game playing.*

Going into dating, I was a bit shell shocked at the games that were played, especially in the London dating arena. Some of my most important values are honesty, integrity and clarity and I felt I was being thrown into a world where anything goes. People playing games by not texting each other, not committing and being open about if and when they wanted to see the person again. It all added up to me feeling played, and left me ungrounded. I started feeling I didn't know who to trust. It was confusing – did he like me or was he purely (or unpurely) trying to get me into bed? Did he want to settle down or have fun? Was he actually busy or was it an excuse to get out of the date or play hard to get? But it doesn't have to be that way. I refused to succumb to the world of game playing and yes, some men I dated did play games, but I didn't want to change me and I knew deep down, that the right person for me wouldn't play games. There are people out there that don't play games, men and women who want to find love, and that think you're amazing just as you are. And you will find them – you will, you really will! I feel passionately that if we were all honest and kind to the people we date, we would all feel happier dating and less like we were throwing ourselves into the lion's den to be eaten. It may be scary to not play games but in return you will attract men that, like you too, don't want to play games but do want to find love.

## Tip Eleven

*Be true to yourself and who you are.* (this links into Tip 10).

It can feel a lot easier to project a certain persona out into the dating world but stop right there! How will we ever find love if we are not our true selves? It will always be a lie and we will always feel a black cloud hanging over us, wondering if we will be found out. I know I did this with projecting a sweet, quiet persona but this is only a part of me – the loud bubbly, strong-minded woman that I am was kept hidden and it felt unauthentic. Not being myself made me feel insecure and it made me attract men who were unable to be with a strong-minded woman, which in turn made me feel like I wasn't good enough. I really don't want for you to make the same mistakes as me. To help you to not make those mistakes, go back over the list you created in 'let's start with loving you' chapter about all the lovely qualities you have and what you can bring to the relationship being yourself and only yourself.

## Tip Twelve

*Be aware of their behaviour.*

Do they call when they say they will? Do they put the effort in? If they do and are still doing so after dating regularly for a few months it sounds like they are keen. If they don't then perhaps it's time to knock it on the head and save your precious time for a man who is committed and wanting to call you and be with you.

## Tip Thirteen

*Avoid getting too intense too quickly.*

This is one I know I struggled with. I really wanted to find love and going from one long term relationship to another to then becoming a serial dater was a complete head mess and I got the whole 'making an effort' thing a bit muddled up. I would want to be a girlfriend way sooner than they were willing to commit. This manifested itself in me cooking for boyfriends (which is fine if it is reciprocated!) and being extra thoughtful about getting their favourite foods in if they were coming over to mine. I remember chatting to one of my single girlfriends at the time who had the following rules: no cooking for them and PJs in bed (no nakedness). I liked these rules and adopted them. When we don't know someone and are trying to make it too serious/intimate too quickly, it feels wrong. There isn't the time to really get to know the person and it can mean that the other person can get scared off of the relationship – I don't want that for you so bear this tip in mind.

## Tip Fourteen

*Keep your dates short.*

Dating can take up a lot of time and so date smart and make

your first dates short dates. Go for a coffee and cake and make plans you can't cancel for later on in the day.

Initially I regularly made the error of turning good first dates into dating marathons: starting off with lunch, going onto a museum, going for dinner and then onto drinks. This all felt too much too soon but the impatient part of me (a very prominent part of me that needs keeping in check!) wanted to carry on and push the date into really knowing the person straight away. What I discovered is that it can be really quite exhausting being on a date for that long – even when you're having fun. I found downtime was needed as dating can take it out of you. It took up massive chunks of my spare time and for men (some of whom I would only see a couple of times) it set the expectations to be high. I would leave the date (as would the guy) thinking that perhaps this person was the elusive 'one', but expectations were raised so high that date two was only ever a bit of a let down. When you see them for short dates, it gives you a chance to think if you like them, reflect on it and then give yourself space to build up anticipation for seeing them again.

So there you go – a few dating tips for being on the date. I found these were the tips I wished I knew when I started out dating, but actually they may not feel quite right for you. The key is listening to what goes on inside you and focusing in on your inner wise leader who can guide you in what the best approach is for you. It's all about empowerment: empowering you to step into your space and own the place you want to carve out for yourself.

## Chapter 10

## Internet dating

Internet dating I feel needs a whole chapter in itself. When I was looking for love, Match.com and Guardian Soulmates were my go to websites. This was before dating apps like Tinder became big – I have drawn on the experience of others with Tinder. Whatever the online channel used for dating, the Internet has opened us up to the possibility of finding love in so many more places than just the local pub and nightclub. This has been great in the sense that it means we have access to a much wider pool of people to search for and connect with to find love, but it also means that we can get into choice overload. It can feel shallow and we can become very picky, dismissing people for the smallest of things. It feeds into our culture of getting everything now and making decisions quickly.

As said, internet dating is great for connecting with a variety of people, but I also found it was overwhelming, very time consuming and something just didn't sit right with me inside. It felt like it fuelled the judgmental, make-a-decision-quick part of me. I felt like I was being judged, and judging without any basis to it, in a flippant way.

## Internet dating

If you are embarking on internet dating, great, make it work for you in the way that honours who you are and the values you hold true. My personal experience of online dating was a rollercoaster. I would sit in front of the laptop replying to messages and find hours would go by online. I felt unsure of the rules on how to deal with not liking someone and what the etiquette to online dating was all about. I had a love/hate relationship – I loved that it gave me excitement in my love life and I felt wanted at points, but it also made me feel not good enough and ungrounded. I regularly reached points of coming offline to have a break and to get my life back.

I learnt a lot from these experiences and wanted to share these tips:

## Tip One

*Be thoroughly true to you.*

Listen to your instinct, listen to your gut and listen to how something feels within you. If something feels wrong or is out of harmony with who you are and who you want to be, then please don't sacrifice you just because everybody else is doing it. I know this is a strange one for the first tip, but internet dating can feel really at odds with who we want to be. Being able to hide behind a screen, being able to dismiss with the swipe of a finger another person, being able to not reply, not respond, say what we like, being able to create a persona that is that little bit more of who we wish we were in real life, all opens up a world of anything goes. A world where who we are can be anything we want and how we behave can go unnoticed and remain anonymous. So when embarking on internet dating, be true to yourself and keep in mind what is important to you. If you feel shaky in this area, please go back over the chapters 'Let's start with loving you' and 'Empowering you to make the most of your life right now'. Having a strong foundation of what is you is fundamental.

## Tip Two

*Your online profile is key.*

My first online profile wasn't getting any hits at all. It was about me but did nothing to 'sell' me and it lacked the fun and playfulness that are at the heart of who I am. My brother took a look through it and helped me draw out the fun, the alternative, the quirky things about me that helped me be more unique in a stack of profiles. It's finding that balance of being who you are in real life and how you are portraying yourself online. It can make us feel like we are not good enough by the very act of not being who we really are portraying online. So ask yourself what do you have to offer a future partner? What are the things that are great and unique about you?

Profiles need to portray who you really are. Ask a couple of close friends or family members what things they love about you. Write down what you want from a partner, and what can you give them. Not in terms of 'good companionship, I am affectionate, I am social' but more paint a picture of what life with you is like. What will being your partner bring to their life? For me, I knew that whoever ended up with me would regularly get to eat yummy cakes and good food. I also knew that I wanted someone I could share my passions of rock climbing, running and snowboarding with. It wasn't key, but it was a big part of me. It's bringing this alive for potential suitors.

Look at the values you uncovered in the first chapter and look at what is true for you. How can you bring this through into your dating profile? What are your dreams and hopes for the future?

Be honest with your profile. Exaggerating the truth, putting up very flattering pictures from years ago all send out a message to yourself that you aren't good enough as you are right now. And you are. You are exactly what someone special is looking for, when you believe it to be so, so will others.

I'm an incredibly open person and had a habit of letting people know everything about me. That didn't help create intrigue and interest in people wanting to find out more about me. So I learnt that holding a little back helped protect me and gradually showed all of me as time went on. This didn't mean I played games, as that goes intrinsically against who I am, but it meant that I protected myself from exposing everything about me to someone I wasn't sure could be trusted with all of me.

## Tip Three

*Avoid game playing.*

Online dating can feel pretty confusing and make you feel vulnerable. You can see when people were last online. If they are online and if they haven't responded to your messaging then it can feel like rejection and make your self-esteem plummet. It can make you feel like the only way around this is to join the game playing, but resist. Remember your values and what you want from your life. Game playing sets a certain tone for whatever comes out of the alliance. If you begin game playing where does it end when you find the right person? It can often make you feel insecure and unsure as to whether they would have fallen for you without the game playing. Instead look at how you can protect yourself but still be authentically you without the game playing. A good place to start with this is creating your own set of rules with how you want to appear online. This can be as simple as being honest and letting people know when things aren't working and you just aren't connecting. Just because others aren't doing that online doesn't mean you can't.

## Tip Four

*Be aware of being too hasty with rejecting profiles and writing people off.*

We can get into a habit of dismissing people, especially if we have seen many profiles before. But you know what, I saw my husband's profile after we married and I definitely would have dismissed and not responded to him online – he wasn't witty with his profile, there were bits of his profile left empty so I would have assumed he didn't care. If I had been single it wouldn't have made me think about contacting him, but how I would have missed out! Sometimes it is hard for a person to express themselves in a witty and light-hearted way and put themself out there, but don't write them off. Listen to your intuition and if you get a nudge to give someone a chance (perhaps there is one that keeps cropping up on searches) maybe it is the universe's way of putting a prospect in front of you.

## Tip Five

*Before you start internet dating give yourself some parameters and boundaries around how much time you want to spend on it.*

Is it an evening a week and a two dates a week, one during the week and one at the weekend? Is it more or is it less? What feels like an amount you want to commit from the outset?

The reason I suggest doing this from the outset is that we can get hooked in and addicted to spending all our time online, responding to emails and messages and searching through the potentials. Initially this can feel fun and exciting but it also adds more weight to the importance of it, and other things in life can fall out of balance easily.

We can get driven by fear we will miss our match if we don't spend every second online. I found with internet dating it was way too easy for me to spend hours looking for love, responding to messages and setting up dates. It was great up to a point but it was also draining. I felt out of balance and ungrounded and would find that things got out of proportion. I got upset if someone hadn't contacted me because I didn't have that balance and perspective. It was completely taking over my life. So limiting it from the outset and being strict with yourself means that you are more than just internet dating and being online. You have a life away from it so that when things happen online (or don't happen) it means it isn't the be all and end all. It's ok as it only makes up one part of your rich and fulfilling life. If you struggle with this, please go back over the life philosophy chapter.

## Tip Six

*Look after yourself.*

Putting yourself out there online can be an incredibly unguarded experience and it can open up a host of vulnerabilities and insecurities within us. People dismissing you immediately and not responding to your message can leave you wondering what you did wrong, questioning how you look and who you are. So now is the time to make sure your self-love and acceptance is high. Get that list out we created in chapter three and pin it somewhere prominent so you can keep reminding yourself of how fantastic you are and how you are a great catch for the right person. Also get your 'pampering me list' out and take action. Schedule in pampering loving treats through the week to keep your love tank full, book in time with friends and family that see and acknowledge your awesomeness. Say to yourself every day in the mirror, 'I love you'. Get your affirmations out – 'I am love, I am whole as I am'.

## Tip Seven

*Take a break.*

It can get overwhelming and feel just too much. Sometimes the best thing to do when you are feeling like this is to take a break from online dating and get back out into the real world. Get in touch with what is important to you. Take the first small step in realising a dream or book a holiday somewhere you've always wanted to visit. And when you feel recharged and ready, dip back in to online dating, knowing you can take a break whenever you want. *You have a choice.*

It can often feel very addictive and I remember feeling like I wanted to keep going because I was sure that my life partner was on a particular dating site somewhere. It was just a matter of me persevering in finding him. Actually, sometimes relinquishing your control and letting it go, knowing and trusting that you don't need to do all the work, trusting that a higher force, the universe, God, whatever you believe in, will guide you to your lifelong partner when the time is right. There is no need to be constantly driving forward to find him. Relax and take a break.

## Tip Eight

*Keep other channels for finding love open as well.*

Because of the huge selection of online dating resources, we can get hooked in to believing and thinking that this is the only way to find love these days. But there are plenty of ways still to find love, and having other options available means you aren't relying purely on internet dating. Go to some singles' events or start a hobby that could open you up to meeting new people. It may not be that you find a man there but a fab new friend who might have a lovely brother you could date. Ask your friends and family if they know of any eligible men they could set you up on dates. Keep all avenues and options open so that internet dating is there as a channel, but it isn't the only one so it has less importance and value attached to it.

## Tip Nine

*Spend time on dates rather than messaging all the time.*

Being behind our laptop or phone typing out witty, flirty responses is safe. Putting yourself out on dates is risky. We actually have to step away from the safety of the laptop and connect in real life, face to face. This can be scary – and is the prime time for insecurities to come up.

I found that when I spent ages messaging back and forth with a person, I would build up a picture in my mind and they would become some sort of perfect man. So it's not surprising when they turned up on the date I was always disappointed, as they never lived up to the perfect story I had created about them. And it wasn't just me that was disappointed: they too had built me up and filled in the blanks to create what they were looking for in a partner, so that when I turned up I never quite matched up to their picture. It would feel like an incredibly large amount of time I had wasted messaging someone that when I met in the flesh, I knew pretty quickly that there was no chemistry there at all. So it's good to message and know more about potential dates, but balance is needed. Just be aware if you are messaging as a way to protect yourself instead of putting yourself out there. Get out there lovely lady and get on some dates!!

## Tip Ten

*Be safe.*

It goes without saying, but let friends or family members know where you are going. Meet in public places with good transport access and ask someone to check you get home ok. Know how you get to and from the place of meeting. It can help to arrange to speak to someone when you leave the date and again when you are home safely. Make sure that you take as many risks out of meeting someone new so that you can enjoy the date without worrying about if you are safe and how you will get home.

So there we have it, a few ways to keep you sane and using internet dating but not having it overrun your life.

## Chapter 11

# Break Up Survival Support – how to survive and be sassier

Breaking up is bloody horrible. It can feel like someone has ripped the ground away from your feet and your once perfect world can feel like a desolate wasteland. This chapter is all around getting you through the aftermath of breaking up.

Break ups can really rock our world. It doesn't matter how long we were with that person – a month, a year, several years, a couple of dates – when we break up with someone we like (or love), it marks the end of a dream, an end of a path. This brings up feelings of loss, mourning and grief as well as anger and hurt, depending on the break up.

My belief is that break ups are there to build us up and make us strong. They show us that we can put up with more that we think we are capable of. You are much stronger than you think you are and you *are* able to bounce back.

I feel in some ways I deserve a prize for the number of break ups I have been through, (as you may do too). The first to shake my world was at university after my first year. I had been dating a tearaway who was a classic 'bad boy'. He was controlling, critical of me and generally not respecting and putting me first. He dumped me by letter addressed to the wrong number in the street, so I ended up calling him up as I hadn't heard from him. He asked me 'have you not received the letter?'. I had to go round to my neighbour, who had opened the letter in error, and pick up this 'Dear John' letter. Wow it was hard to take and hard to read. I believed we had had fun, I could (crazily) see a future, despite the fact he made me miserable and put me down. I remember before we broke up thinking to myself when I was out with him and his friends in Brighton, 'Is this the most miserable I can possibly be?' I knew the relationship kept me small and fuelled my insecurities, but like a moth to the flame, I was drawn in and wanted his attention and elusive love. He dumped me as he didn't have time to have a girlfriend *'and'* practise on his DJ decks. I was heartbroken, lost and dazed. I cried inconsolably and didn't know quite what to do with myself. I was sad for weeks. I got a part-time job to bring in money (I was in the university holidays and needed cash). I can't remember much about that time but I remember the pain of having my heart broken. I remember coming across a book that had a monumental impact on me and my life: *Feel The Fear And Do It Anyway* by Susan Jeffers and by reading this and relying on some amazing friends, I started to find my feet.

This first dating experience of heartache taught me some strategies that I finessed over the years of breaking up and I want to share these with you to empower and support you through the rubbish and utter misery of being dumped.

## Break up but better

## 1. Look after yourself.

It sounds simple but good self-care and self-love are key – this is the time to remember you are amazing. Just because someone doesn't recognise or want to be with your particular type of amazingness doesn't take away from the fact that you are one hundred per cent A-mazing.

Get out your list of all the things that are amazing about you and remind yourself that your package of loveliness is there to be discovered by your special someone. I was reminded by a colleague that how seeing the rejection from dating as a non-personal experience can really help. This was brought to life for me in the following analogy: if you are trying to get an art gallery to exhibit your art, they may reject it not because your art isn't any good, but because their art gallery is all about a specific type of art and yours doesn't match what they are looking for. Like art, we too are specific, and just because someone doesn't want to be with us doesn't mean we aren't an amazing piece of art. It just means we aren't the art for that particular gallery. But there will be a gallery (or partner) out there for us.

## 2. Have an SOS list on the ready.

This list is full of all the things you can do to get you back on track, be it eating a massive amount of raw cake mix (one of my favourites), watching your favourite movies, bubble baths, nice walks, hanging out with nurturing friends. Whatever it takes to make you feel good, do it! Hard as it may feel, looking after yourself, treating yourself to something, anything that puts a smidgen of light into your day is a must.

## 3. Create a 'what I loved' and 'what I won't miss' list.

Be honest, when you were dating your ex were there things about him you weren't so keen on? Were there traits he possessed, ways he behaved, attitudes he had that didn't quite gel with you and who you are? Start writing a list of things you won't miss. Also write a list of everything you will miss about your ex. Write it all down. Perhaps he was really funny, a great cook or really adventurous and exciting. Whatever it is you loved about him, write it down. I found that writing down all the things that were good and bad helped me see that actually it's all a balance, and acknowledging the things I would miss was honouring what dreams, hopes and aspirations (no matter how short lived) I had for this relationship.

## 4. Have a massive declutter.

I love a good declutter and now is the time to declutter everything that reminds you of him, be it a memento of a day trip or holiday you had together or an outfit you chose when you were with him. Everything that reminds you in some way, shape or form of him, remove and declutter. This could be giving away to friends and family or charity. The act of throwing it away in a big bin liner can be very therapeutic. When I did this it helped me reclaim me again. My energy wasn't being drawn to things that reminded me of him, so I felt better. I thought of the ex less and I felt it cleansed me.

## 5. Cry, wail, sob.

Do whatever you need to express the pain inside and connect in with that pain. Having a supply of sad movies and a sad song playlist are great ways to tap into the pain and allowing it all to come out rather than being stuffed down deep inside.

## 6. Take time out just for you.

This sounds clichéd but it takes time to feel less pain over the hurt you've gone through, so cut yourself some slack, take some holiday from work and allow yourself to be sad. When we carry on as if nothing has happened and put a brave face on, the pain and hurt are still there within us, but are hidden away. They find a way to come out. So take time out and put you first.

## 7. Create a calendar of events.

Often we can have a tendency to look back at our relationship and our ex with rose-tinted glasses which makes us feel worse not better – and I am all about helping you to feel better. So get a pen and paper and jot down the days, weeks, months of your relationship in a calendar and mark on when there were good times and when there were bad events or things that weren't going so well. We all have a tendency to look at relationships that have ended through rose-tinted glasses, but often they aren't quite so rosy. When I actually went over my diary with one ex in my early twenties, I was quite taken aback – all the times I thought were glowing were in fact intermingled with lots of bad times and miserable times – was my mind deceiving me? How had I forgotten most of this pain and heartache? When I did this the first time it was a real eye opener and I was quite frankly amazed we'd lasted as long as we did. I was frustrated with myself for not getting rid of the loser but instead waiting to be dumped (at this stage I had major self-acceptance and love work needed). So jot down your experience. If you have a journal – even better. Look over it and write in the good and bad times and you may well be surprised that seeing it in chronological order, it isn't quite so rosy as the rose-tinted glasses would have you believe.

## 8. Create a 'break up but better' song list.

Use this to play and remind you of your amazing self. Play it on your iPod to remind you of all the amazing things about you and that you will survive! Speaking of which, that was a song on my breakup but better playlist. To get a few other playlist ideas take a look in the box below.

---

Break-up tunes
Gloria Gaynor – 'I Will Survive'
Glee – 'Survive' medley
Cher – 'Believe'
Sugababes – 'Stronger'
Glee cast – 'Forget You'

---

> Beyoncé – 'Irreplaceable'
> Anastacia – 'Left Outside Alone'

## 9. Write a letter to your ex but don't post it.

Use the letter to get your thoughts out about the ex and as a means to voice the upset and pain you have felt. Either put it somewhere safe, or burn it.

## 10. Don't sleep with your ex.

I did this once when a long-term relationship ended and it was a BIG mistake. I still wanted it to work. Sex in a relationship feels so different to when you are breaking up with someone or being broken up with. It feels sad. You ask yourself things like 'Why aren't they hugging you for so long afterwards?' It feels confusing. You analyse everything. Does this mean we are back together? It gives glimmers of hope and with your already-hurt heart, what you need is distance and no contact with this ex so that you can fully heal and mend.

## 11. Connect with your friends and family.

I had a few amazing girlfriends who were just there in a crisis to make me laugh and to get me out of the slump. I was also blessed with my amazing family. My dad would give incredibly insightful readings on the ex in question. My ever-caring and loving mum mopped up the tears and provided a world full of love. My brother and sister would drop everything to listen and pick up the pieces of the heartache.

They all helped me to recover and were my support network. Research shows that having a strong support network is key in building your resilience. And when breaking up and picking yourself back up, you certainly need to draw on your resilience. Let your friends and family know that you may need more support to get through this and that you may need to lean on them more. This prepares them for calls at times in the night when you are extra sad.

## 12. Start creating a list of all the things you can do now you are not in that relationship.

This was something I had never thought of. After one of my break ups I stumbled across another amazing book called *It's A Breakup Not A Breakdown* by Lisa Steadman which got me thinking about changing the focus of my thinking: not just focusing on the loss but actually looking at the delicious freedom and patting myself on my back for dodging a potentially-fatal relationship bullet.

## 13. Have faith in the bigger picture.

You may or may not believe in something other than this earth and this moment, but for me believing in fate, the universe and spiritual guides out there helping me on my way gave, and still gives, me comfort that things will work out for my higher good. And that no matter what that higher good is, in the words of Susan Jeffers – 'I'll handle it!' When I felt that what I was experiencing was part of some bigger plan for me, it gave me faith and hope that it would all be all right in the end, and that this challenge (of heartache) was here to teach me something special. Which leads me on to...

## 14. What have you learnt?

How have you grown from this experience? When we look for the meaning and purpose and appreciate what we learnt by being in a relationship, it helps turn us over to gratitude. I'm not saying this is easy initially and I can hear you shout: 'but he was a swine and she is asking me to be grateful for this?!' But hang on a second before you think I am crazy! Every experience we have teaches us something and gives us an opportunity to learn and grow and change.

We have a choice about how we approach it and how we choose to approach it. When we go through the same rubbish situations over and over again, it is often our clue that we are just not getting the lesson and so need to repeat the experience again until we do. So some of the lessons and things I was grateful for included getting to see new places and have my eyes open to new experiences, being introduced to new films or music I had never considered, being taught new recipes I could add to my repertoire of meals and being told I was ugly in some way (breasts, hair and bottom were usually the places of vulnerability). This last one let me realise that my self-love must be low to allow the ex to be so critical of me.

## 15. Throw yourself a moving on party.

This again I learnt from the *It's A Breakup Not A Breakdown* book and my goodness did I throw myself a great party. I had just moved into my first studio flat after being dumped by a man I believed at the time was my soulmate. I was low and sad, in London with no friends nearby, but this new home was an amazing gift from the universe (and funnily enough the history of the flat indicated that many a woman retreated there to create a haven for herself and build herself up). This space enabled me to invite my amazing friends round. I put on a beautiful purple dress (that I had bought for a wedding I ended up not going to due to the breakup) and we made raspberry mojitos in my metre-square kitchenette, danced to happy songs and I saw it as an opportunity to be out with the old and in with the sassy new. If you have been through a break up and are now at the stage to hang up the misery and grief and move on, then I can highly recommend marking the occasion by inviting your friends over for a shindig of sorts to launch you back into the world.

## 16. Do something for yourself.

Do this purely for yourself, because you can – you are free and single and amazing! Through my breakups, I booked travelling trips I had only ever dreamed of, I got my hair cut short, I tried out new restaurants, I ventured to the cinema on my own, I got braces and I booked myself in for massages. I did whatever I needed to do to get me back on track and help me put the relationship behind me.

## 17. Avoid the wallow world.

It is *very* easy to fall into the trap of wallowing over what has passed and what you are missing out on. I fell into this trap briefly and it felt rubbish. I felt worse, not better, in wallow world. I focused on the bad and sad and the misery and 'Miss Drama Queen' that I can sometimes be saw no end and no way out. What I learnt is that we all have a choice about how we handle certain situations. We can either wallow or we can pick ourselves up and dust ourselves off and start again. We can all do it. It's purely our choice which way we choose to turn.

Wallowing on what we've lost has its place. It's necessary so that you get in the emotion – feel it and then move on. But sometimes it can feel like a place that's here to stay and it's when you are in the midst of wallow world and have been there a while then this tip is for you.

We have this one life to do with it what we wish. If your ninety-five-year-old self was looking back over your life and at this particular breakup, what would that self say to you? What chink of positivity and hope can you find in what has happened? What can you do to make yourself feel a little bit better? Focusing on what is good in your life is a great way of feeling better.

There we have it, some ways to empower you to experience and survive your break ups.

So a run through:

- ♥ Look after yourself
- ♥ Have an SOS kit
- ♥ Create a 'what I loved' and 'will miss' and 'what I won't miss' list
- ♥ Declutter
- ♥ Cry, wail, sob
- ♥ Take time out for you
- ♥ Create a calendar of events
- ♥ Create a break up but better playlist

Break Up Survival Support – how to survive and be sassier

- ♥ Write a letter
- ♥ Don't sleep with your ex
- ♥ Connect with friends and family
- ♥ Create a list of all the things you can do now that you're not in a relationship
- ♥ Have faith in the bigger picture
- ♥ Write down all that you have learnt from the relationship – how can you grow
- ♥ Throw a moving on party
- ♥ Do something purely for yourself
- ♥ Avoid the wallow world of misery.

## Afterword

We've come to the end of the book, we have worked on how to build you up to love yourself, be strong when life throws challenges your way and how to create the life you love.

I hope you have found the book has helped you flourish as much as the tools have helped me to.

I would love to hear how you get on with the exercises and tools in the book and let me know on my Facebook page, Jenniferboon Coaching, how you are creating a life you love and loving the stage you are in.

I believe we all go through experiences to teach us something so we grow as a person and on a soul level. I hope this book has empowered you to listen to your inner wisdom, be strong in your beliefs and know that as someone special there will be an amazing man out there for you. That someone is there and is sitting wondering where on earth you are. You will meet at the time that is right for the both of you, but until that happens, know that this time in your life has been sent to you for you to make the most of. So set about creating the life you love, follow your heart, do things you only ever dreamed of in your wildest dreams so that when your true love comes along you are ready, really ready to commit whole-heartedly. Ready to share your life and ready to start the next phase of your life and new adventure with no regrets of not making the most of being single.

Good luck, Love Jennifer x

## Acknowledgements

This book would not have come into fruition without the support and love from my soulmate, Si. You gave me hope, bolstered me when I was unsure about writing this and as always, supported me in growing into the person I want to be. Thank you for loving me and accepting me so completely. You are and always will be my one true love.

Thank you to Wendy for getting me through the editing process and giving me the energy boost to bring this book to completion.

Julia, my book buddy, thank you for encouraging this and checking in weekly for word count updates – I appreciate it.

For my family and friends who have been there through the years, supporting me through the highs and lows – thank you.

And a final big thank you to all the dates I have had and failed relationships – without you I wouldn't be the person I am today. Thank you for building my resilience, showing me I am made of more than I thought I was and for helping me love myself enough to wait for my one true love. I wish you all well.